MANAGEMENT FAILURES

LESSONS LEARNED THROUGH CASE STUDY

Joshua D. Jensen, EdD, MBA, MPA
Samuel L. Dunn, PhD, DBA, MBA
William J. Russell, JD, MBA

ISBN EBOOK: 978-1-7366318-4-3
ISBN PAPERBACK: 978-1-7366318-5-0

Cover design by:
Alyssa N. Jensen

Printed in the USA

TABLE OF CONTENTS

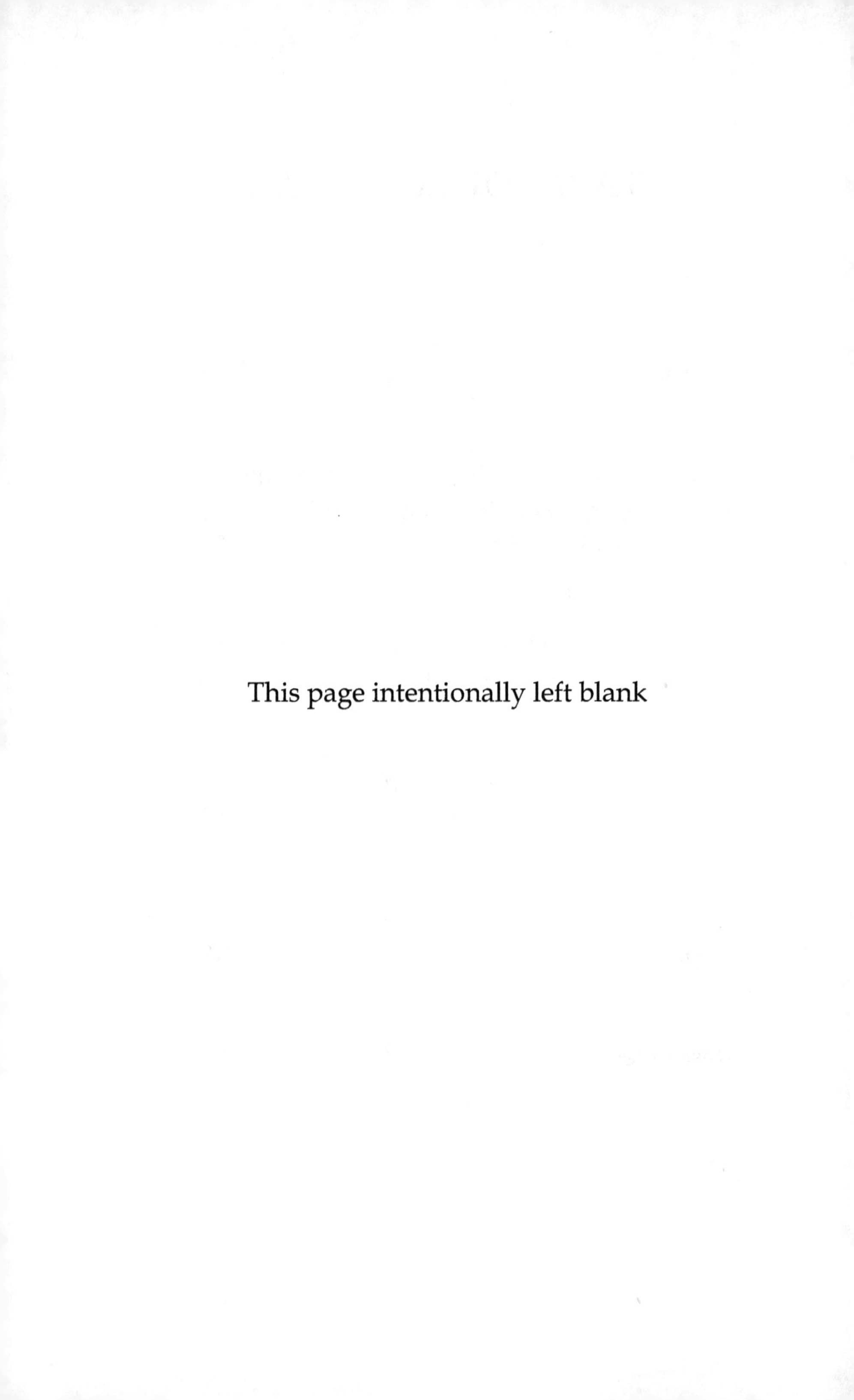

This page intentionally left blank

FOREWARD

Our 21st century global business environment consists of a very complex and challenging landscape. Businesses rise, and businesses fall. Businesses thrive, and businesses stall. What determines the success or failure of a business? Well, there are many things, but one thing is for sure: management plays a critical role in the success of any business.

Management is messy. There is no one nice and neat resource that can adequately prepare a manager for what they will experience throughout their career. **Management is challenging**. There is no single, straightforward management handbook to reference. Perhaps one can learn the basics in an undergraduate management degree program. Even better, one can learn advanced strategies and insights in a graduate management degree program. These programs will no doubt equip one to be the best manager they can possibly be. But at the end of the day, experience is where the rubber hits the road – where a manager will ultimately rise or fall. Managers learn more by doing and experiencing than by studying. Furthermore, mangers learn just as much, if not more, from their failures as they do their successes.

For over two years now, the COVID-19 pandemic has persisted. In the United States, over 900,000 people have died due to COVID-related illnesses – there have been more than 5.74 million deaths worldwide. In addition to the pandemic wreaking havoc in the personal lives of people around the world, it has also wreaked havoc throughout the global business environment. One word to describe the pandemic's impact on business would be **disruptive**. Organizations have been disrupted, and in many ways have been forced to find new and different ways of doing things. Through creativity and innovation, some organizations have been able to pivot and adapt their business model to the current business environment. Many of these organizations have actually experienced greater success despite the pandemic. Other organizations however, weren't up to the challenge and due to their inability to pivot and respond appropriately to the pandemic, ended up flailing or failing. Overall, the pandemic has taught us many business lessons, but one of the greatest lessons learned is this: managers today must be able to effectively lead organizations and people through adversity, chaos, and uncertainty.

This book contains stories of failure - management failures. While not all business failures are the result of poor management, a good number of them are. This book contains a series of accounts where managers have failed - failed to make good decisions, failed to address organizational issues, failed to address interpersonal issues, as well as a host of other failures. While all failures don't lead to the collapse of a business, all failures have some measurable impact on the people and the organizations in which the failure touched.

The purpose of this book is not to commiserate with managers, embarrass them, or feel sorry for managers that have blown it. Rather, experience is a master teacher, and the goal of this book is to help managers learn from the mistakes and failures of others. In this book the authors present a series of stories - case studies if you will - that cover a broad range of complex business situations. The intent of each case study is to present you with management issues and failures, get you to think critically about the management issues and failures, and provide guidance on how to avoid similar failures in your management practice.

Made specially to complement undergraduate and graduate courses in management and leadership, this book is organized in a series of "case studies." Each case study presents a situation or scenario, poses discussion questions for reflection and analysis, and then includes expert analysis by the authors of the key issues of the case and recommendations for how the failure could have been avoided.

While some of the stories presented are globally-known failures that were reported through major media outlets, most of the stories come straight from the authors' combined 125 years of management experience. Some of the failure you will read about are failures of the authors. Others are failures that the authors experienced or witnessed first-hand. Nonetheless, the authors have learned so much throughout their experiences, and they are eager to share their insights with you throughout this book. We are confident that this book will prove to be a valuable resource in your management toolbox.

This page intentionally left blank

CHAPTER ONE

MISTAKES AND FAILURES

This page intentionally left blank

Introduction

We all have made mistakes, and we all have failed at some point in our life. Not only do we as individuals make mistakes, but groups of us in companies make mistakes as well. Failure is a part of life; it can't be avoided.

Mistakes and failures come in all shapes and sizes. One is tempted to use the language of sin: some failures are "cardinal sins" and have disastrous consequences, with much negative fallout for the people and/or the companies involved. Sometimes the consequences are fatal. Then there are the failures that would be categorized as "venial sins" – mistakes and failures that are little or small and have few negative results.

Sometimes mistakes and failures arise because the person or firm took some positive-intended action that brought trouble to the people involved. Sometimes they occur because a person in authority did *not* take the action they should have taken. Sometimes failures occur because of the actions of a third party, such as the government or other regulatory authority. In other words, the source of failure may be personal, or it may be internal or external to the company; sources are explored further below.

Before we go any further, it is appropriate to provide definitions for these two terms. From the online *Oxford Dictionary,* we have the following:

> Failure (Noun). 1. Lack of success; 2. The neglect or omission of expected or required action; 3. The action or state of not functioning; 4. The collapse of

a business.

Also, from the *Oxford Dictionary* we have:

> Mistake (Noun). 1. An act or judgement that is misguided or wrong. 2. Something, especially a word, figure, or fact, which is not correct; an inaccuracy.

We will be using these two terms throughout the duration of this book.

Case Studies of Failure

In Chapters 2, 3, and 4 of this book you will find a number of case studies - scenarios of mistakes and failures. There are several cases of failure that have occurred in large, well-known companies. Chapter 2 focuses on these large, for-profit companies as well as some cases from governmental entities. Chapter 3 focuses on small, for-profit firms, and Chapter 4 focuses on not-for-profit firms of various sizes. Most of the case studies in this book come from the vast experiences of the three authors, whose combined careers represent over 125 years of management experience. In these cases, the names of the principals and participants, the names of the companies and cities, and minor details have been changed to protect the reputations of the companies and people involved.

You will find stories of problems that had a significant impact on the company involved; in some the company discussed was forced to close and thousands of people suffered the consequences. In other situations where the problem arose from one person, the person involved was fired because of his or her actions, and not much other damage was done.

Following each case study, you will find a short list of discussion questions. These questions can be used for case study analysis for management training and leadership development. Finally, the authors include an analysis section that includes expert opinion on what management mistakes were made and how they can be avoided in the future.

Chapter 5, the closing chapter, is a reprise of the cases and anecdotes of mistakes and failures that were discussed throughout the previous chapters of the book.

Various Contexts of Failures

Failure comes in all sizes, shapes and forms. Failure has many contexts. In this section we describe and expand on some of the various contexts from which failures emerge.

Failure in For-Profit Companies

Failures happen in for-profit companies, large and small. A for-profit college that failed was ITT, based in Indianapolis, Indiana. At the time of its closure, ITT Educational Services had 130 campuses around the country and 43,000 students. Another big for-profit firm that failed was the movie rental firm Blockbuster Video, which took bankruptcy in 2010 and closed its remaining 300 stores in 2013.

Failure in Not-for-Profit Companies

Failures occur in not-for-profit organizations, both big and small. A big non-profit that completely failed was the Federal Employment Guidance Service (FEGS). This New York organization had 120,000 household clients, almost 2,000 employees, and a $250M annual budget. When the FEGS closed in 2015 it had nearly $50M in debts and liabilities.

Failure in Fortune 500 Huge Companies

One famous failure, the subject of much discussion in business classes, was the introduction by Ford Motor Company of the Edsel car. The 1958 model year Edsel was introduced in late 1957 and continued through 1960. Ford lost an estimated $350M on the venture.

Failure in Mom-and-Pop Companies

Mom-and-pop firms make mistakes, often because of their limited knowledge of business practices. Consider the case of JoMarv's Grocery, a small mom-and-pop grocery store in the Hispanic district of Milwaukee. JoMarv's store hours for 30 years had been from 7am until 9pm. Marvin Garcia noticed the average number of customers after 8pm was low, so he decided to close at 8pm instead of 9pm. After a year with the new hours Marv noticed there were few customers after 7pm, so he decided to close the store at 7pm. The next year he noticed that the store now had fewer customers after 6pm, so he closed at 6pm. Overall JoMarv's had a significant decrease in net profits over the three-year period it was changing its hours. Marv got several complaints about the new hours from long-time customers.

Failure Arising from Unethical Behavior

Some failures are personal more than institutional and arise from the unethical behavior of a particular individual. Consider the case of Marjorie Whipple. She was the accountant in a small firm in Dayton, Ohio. She was responsible for all funds coming into the firm, for the bank accounts, for paying bills, and she was handling the payroll. She discovered a way she could take small amounts of the money that was coming in for her personal use. This behavior went on for six years during which time she embezzled an estimated $83,000. She was eventually caught when the IRS audited the firm's tax returns and the CEO, in preparation for the IRS, hired an outside accounting firm to audit the firm's books. Whipple was fired, but no charges were brought against her.

Failure from Criminal Activity

Still other failures arise from intentional criminal activity. Consider the Tylenol case in which a person or persons unknown put cyanide in Tylenol capsules after the pills left the factory. It was reported that seven people died from taking the adulterated capsules. Johnson & Johnson, the parent company, faced a deadly problem and a public relations setback that could have seriously wounded the company.

Companies make mistakes and have failures, but often the company can correct the problem and weather the storm. In the Tylenol case the company announced to the public the problem with the capsules, then immediately pulled an estimated 18 million

Tylenol bottles from the shelves at an estimated cost of $18M. Johnson & Johnson then worked to make sure the problem was resolved. The reaction of the public was very positive and Tylenol emerged with its good reputation intact. Johnson & Johnson's handling of the crisis is cited often in management books as a great example of a firm doing the right thing in the face of a company disaster. The firm's reaction was an example of effective crisis management. It is noted that the recovery operations are always critical to the long-term health of the firm, for a firm's reaction to an untoward situation can cause more difficulty than the original problem.

Failure from Revolt of the Employees

Employees may revolt and cause failure. John Anderson was CFO of Miltand Industries, Inc. He was well liked by the CEO and the board, but was despised by the rank-and-file employees. When the CEO retired the board appointed Anderson to be the new CEO. The employee union took the unusual step of protesting Anderson's appointment. When that brought no action, the union called a strike, even though the strike violated the union agreement. After four days of the strike, the board relented and rescinded Anderson's appointment as CEO.

Failure from Board Inaction

Sometimes there are failures because the CEO or the Board of Directors did not take charge and do the hard work required. David Whitsun was the CEO of one such firm. He had been CEO for eight years and done a reasonably good job, as viewed by the board - a pass-through board. Then Whitsun appeared to have a mid-life crisis. He divorced his wife, bought a huge yacht, and started spending much of his time in Las Vegas, that is, when he wasn't on his yacht in Cancún. This change in life negatively influenced his work, which was evident within six months of his divorce. The board took no action, and let Whitsun continue his wayward ways for four years. Then Whitsun quit as CEO. In the meantime, the firm had lost considerable ground, its stock value was down by 28%, sales were down by 17%, and there was generally bad morale in the firm. An offer came to buy the firm; at that point the board decided to sell and get out.

Failure from Poor Planning

Some failures come from poor planning. Rogers Metallurgical Company bid for a project to provide 20,000 metal hasps to Knighthorn Integrators. The contract had a due date with high penalties for failure to deliver the hasps. The biggest order for hasps Rogers had ever had in the past was for 3,000 hasps. Trying to produce 20,000 in the timeframe promised was like guaranteeing the moon to Napoleon. Rogers failed to deliver and was socked with a $200,000 penalty. Rogers couldn't produce and declared bankruptcy.

Failure from Poor Management Practices

Poor understanding of management principles may lead to failure. The CEO and Board of Directors of Jenkins Cloth and Steel decided to expand the firm's operations. The firm was doing okay, but not stellar.

Profits were running at about 3% on annual sales of $35M. To expand, the firm needed a new building that would cost about $20M. The firm was able to talk a local bank into lending that much money to the firm, so the firm moved ahead with the new building. Debt service on the loan was about $1M per year, which overwhelmed the firm. The company's reserves were spent down in three years, and then the company defaulted on its building payments. The bank took back the building. Two years later Jenkins went bankrupt and closed.

Failure to Understand the Changing Environment

Quite often, failures are caused by a firm that misunderstands the changing world. Consider the Rutgers Telecom Company, a regional telephone service company in Kentucky. Rutgers' management refused to endorse the use of cell phones for fear it would cannibalize its landline customers. Over time, the number of Rutgers' landline customers dwindled, and eventually Rutgers was bought out by a national telecommunications firm.

Failure Caused by Personality Deficiencies

Failures may occur because the person in charge is not equipped by personality to make hard decisions. An example was Marvin Jones, a good old boy who had been with his firm for 25 years. He worked his way up from stock-picker to head of the HR department. Everybody liked good old Marvin. When the CEO retired, the board picked Marvin to be the new CEO. In his first year Marvin made some tough decisions that made a bunch of the employees mad. This frustrated Marvin so much that he quit making hard decisions. He let the company drift, until finally things got so bad the board realized Marvin was not the right person to be CEO, and Marvin was let go.

Failure Caused by Rogue Employees

Another failure may occur caused by a single employee who commits an offense while on the job, or by an employee who does wrong while not on the job but the employee is publicly identified with the company. In such a case the firm may attempt to defend itself by saying that it did not initiate nor approve the employee's action, and the firm's management had no knowledge that such bad behavior was occurring. Such a defense may or may not come to the firm's rescue, for it may be pointed out that the firm *should* have known about the problem and did not take steps in advance to mitigate the risk. In other words, the firm had an environment and a culture which allowed or encouraged the bad activity.

An example of an employee causing harm was the 1984 Union Carbide case out of Bhopal, India. Allegedly, an employee introduced water into a tank of methyl isocyanate, causing a chemical reaction that led the tank to leak the deadly chemical across the city of Bhopal. Allegedly as many as 16,000 people were killed and as many as 200,000 injured as a result of the leak. There are stories of an exceptional number of mentally and physically disabled children being born in the area. Lawsuits over the disaster continue to this day.

Failure Caused by Suppliers

In 1997 one of Toyota's main suppliers had a fire that allegedly cost Toyota $195M in disruption costs and $325M in sales losses. The fire was at the Aisin Seiki firm in Kariya, Japan. That firm was the main supplier of brake valves that Toyota used in many of its assembly plants in Japan.

Failure Caused by Disasters

In 2013 there was a fire at the Citgo Oil Refinery in Lemont, Illinois. The fire was traced to a faulty fitting. Refinery production was shut down for nine months. The maintenance company had to pay $456M in damages for lost profits and repair damages.

Taking Risks

When considering mistakes and failures one must put those in the context of taking risks. An aggressive company takes risks regularly. Developing a new product, expanding into a new country, buying out another firm, merging, getting a new CEO, spinning off a subsidiary, and listing on the stock market – all these are risks. A company which is not taking some risks is probably one doomed to fail downstream.

A well-managed company takes risks, but it does so with its eyes wide open. All aspects of the proposed venture are considered: budgets, personnel, products, reputation, as well as the impact on current products, potential customers, supply chains, and potential profits. Probability analysis is often used. Then there's the old smell test. After all risks have been assessed and mitigated as appropriate, the CEO and board must decide whether to go ahead and take the risk knowing full well there may be a failure, or whether to drop the initiative. A percentage, hopefully low, of the risks will lead to failure; some failure is expected.

There are various magnitudes of risks, some big and high-stakes, and some small and inconsequential. Taking a big risk may be betting the company on a particular outcome. A small risk may be betting the job of just a few people, or betting on the future of a company division.

A friend of one of the authors had an idea for a new product in his firm. He needed some seed money to get the product launched, only $25,000. He went to the CEO and asked for the money. He told the CEO the product would be a success; if it wasn't the CEO could fire him. The CEO thought about the prospects, gave approval, and the employee was off and running. The product turned out to be a big success and established the reputation of the employee. Several years later that some employee became CEO of the firm.

Mitigating and Managing Risk

Management failures at all levels create risks that can threaten the viability or even the existence of the organization. Some risks can be mitigated. Other risks cannot be anticipated in advance but can be managed to minimize impact on the business.

Companies can mitigate risk in advance by taking action that will head off trouble before it occurs, or help resolve problems after they occur. Perhaps insurance may be obtained that will cover untoward eventualities. The following are practical approaches to mitigating or managing the risks that can attend management failures.

Activist Boards

Most corporations are required by law to have a board of directors. The board is the ultimate authority on the direction and management of the firm. The board employs and directs the work of the CEO. Above all, the board should closely monitor the work of the CEO and the CFO.

Since the board is legally responsible for the firm, the board must take control and be involved with the running of the firm. This doesn't mean the board micromanages the firm; the board sets the general direction, determines major policies, and holds the CEO responsible for managing the firm in a manner congruent with board policy. The rub here is that the board is held accountable financially and legally for the actions of the firm. Any untoward direction of the firm may result in lawsuits against the board collectively and board members individually. The corporate umbrella does not always protect individual board members.

In many small firms the boards are passive. Board members may be relatives or friends of the owner(s) of the firm, one of which is typically the CEO. These boards, known as pass-through boards, confirm the actions of the CEO and don't use professional expertise to control the CEO's actions. In essence, the CEO has free-reign to do as he or she pleases, since the board will rubber-stamp the CEO's actions.

In large corporations the problem of the pass-through board is not so prevalent. Board members are often voted into their positions by the shareholders. Often board members are compensated for their work.

However, even large companies have trouble with pass-through boards. Consider the situation of the Boeing Company with its 737 difficulties. Boeing was sued by some shareholders who stated that the former CEO Dennis Muilenburg misled what the plaintiffs portray as a largely passive board. Directors also allegedly were preoccupied by negative news stories, failing to press management over specific MAX engineering problems and skipping meetings focused on safety, according to the 142-page lawsuit (Tangel & Pasztor, 2020, pp. A1-A5).

Insurance Coverage

One-way organizations can mitigate risk and provide protection from mistakes and failures is through insurance. Companies purchase insurance to cover losses, potential or actual, of various kinds. Here are some common insurance policies for businesses:

Directors and Officers (D&O) Insurance. Directors and officers of the firm need insurance to provide protection in case one or more is sued for misdeeds of omission or commission. This might cover real or alleged wrongful acts such as fraud, breach of fiduciary responsibility, or failure to comply with laws. D&O insurance will not only cover liability determined to exist, but may also include coverage for the costs (attorney's fees, expert witness fees, costs of depositions, copying and travel, among others) of the legal defense of the directors and officers in the event of a lawsuit.

Errors and Omissions (E&O) Coverage. You may give bad advice to a client, miss a deadline, install materials incorrectly, or cause harm in other ways. A recent problem came from hackers who held a firm's computer services for ransom, causing clients of that company to lose business. Those clients may sue the firm for damages. Errors and omission coverage may assist you in covering the damage. It may also cover legal costs to defend your firm against unwarranted accusations.

Professional (Malpractice) Insurance. You may have employees in your firm who have special risks because of their professional practices. Ordinary D&O insurance may not cover professional failures. Medical doctors, attorneys, accountants, psychologists, and rehabilitation specialists come to mind as examples of this type of employee. This category of employees may need specialized insurance coverage.

General Liability Insurance. Negligent or tortious conduct (intentional or otherwise) in business operations may lead to legal liability resulting from losses to a person or organization who is damaged by virtue of the negligent or tortious conduct. The damage (or loss) may involve personal injury, property damage, medical payments, lost earnings, legal costs or an array of other possible losses. General coverage for all liability (and costs of defense) for all types of losses is referred to as General Liability or Comprehensive General Liability coverage.

Product Liability Insurance. If you manufacture or sell a product, and if that product turns out to be defective, and if somebody is harmed and suffers loss because of the product defect, you may be held liable. This often leads to a damage lawsuit. Product Liability Insurance may provide coverage for this sort of risk.

Property Insurance. If property owned by a person or organization is damaged by any one of a myriad of causes (weather, natural disaster, vandalism, arson and others) the person or firm will suffer economic loss because of the damage to the property. Property Insurance provides coverage for this sort of loss.

Automobile Insurance. If a person or firm owns or operates cars, trucks or rolling stock of any sort, losses from the ownership or operation of the vehicles can be covered by Automobile Insurance. Note that General Liability Insurance and Property Insurance typically exclude losses involving vehicles. Thus, it is necessary to purchase separate coverage for the vehicles, both liability and property insurance.

Business Interruption Insurance. You need protection in case business is interrupted because of a fire, or sabotage.

Crime Insurance. If a person or firm suffers a loss by virtue of crime, separate coverage must be in place for crime losses. An example would be extortion or embezzlement by an employee. Neither General

Liability nor Property Insurance cover crime losses. It is necessary to purchase separate insurance for this sort of loss.

<u>Cyber Coverage</u>. Today there are many sorts of losses that occur by virtue of the role of computers and the internet in all that we do. Many sorts of losses that may occur in the cyber world are not covered by other types of insurance. This may include data loss, cyber-attacks, viruses, and others. It may be necessary to purchase separate insurance for this sort of loss.

<u>Exclusions</u>. Be very careful to determine what is covered and what is not covered in your various insurance policies. Many policies will not cover criminal activity, acts of God, or warfare. Check especially for terrorism coverage. Also, make sure your firm is forthcoming with relevant information when it applies for the insurance coverage. The *Wall Street Journal* reported on March 30, 2018 that "A South Korean insurance company denied a claim by a cryptocurrency exchange that suffered a cyberattack in December." The parent company of the cryptocurrency exchange said the insurance company "had accused it of trying to rush getting its insurance and failing to disclose important information while negotiating the policy."

<u>Deductibles and Limits of Liability</u>. Most insurance policies contain two common elements: Deductibles and Limits of Liability. A deductible is the amount that the person or firm will be responsible to pay before insurance coverage begins. Usually a policy with a higher deductible is less expensive to purchase. A

person or organization should buy coverage with as high a deductible as they can reasonable manage in ordinary operations, assuming that a loss will be experienced, and perhaps multiple losses. The Limit of Liability is the maximum amount that an insurer will pay on any loss. It is possible in most cases to buy as high a limit of liability as is needed to protect the person or firm.

Proactive Legal Counsel

Many management failures might be avoided if management consults with, and listens to, legal counsel. Attorneys are aware of laws, cases, regulations, and other business practice matters that are particularly risky. Every active manager should have access to legal counsel (and should consider this a necessary business expense, to be built into every business model or plan) in order to minimize risks that may lurk outside of the field of vision of the manager.

Many managers perceive attorneys to be impediments to doing what they want to get done. If this is true, it is because the attorney is trained to see a problem or risk that is outside the scope of expertise of the manager. Attorneys normally do not tell managers what they can or cannot do; the manager is always free to ignore the attorney. Attorneys do tell managers what might happen if they elect to take a certain course of action. Managers ignore legal counsel at their own risk.

Empowered Management Team

Many management failures occur by virtue of what might be called the "Lone Ranger" syndrome. It is almost always true that two minds can produce a better vision than one mind. Many managers are self-confident, as they should be, but also reject input from their colleagues or subordinates. And those colleagues or subordinates often see trouble coming around the bend while the manager is focused on the road directly ahead. The power of multiple perspectives cannot be denied.

Fewer failures will occur for any manager if she or he will simply make it clear to those around that manager (employees, subordinates, supervisors, board of director members or even family) that they can bring him or her thoughts, comments, warnings, insights and information without any fear, whatsoever, of adverse reaction. Moreover, the manager needs to listen. The airing of perceived problems by others is NOT insubordination or mutiny. The manager needs to see such support as necessary and helpful. That does not mean that the manager does not make the ultimate decision. However, it does mean that the manager surveys an entire field of vision before making that decision.

Policies

Make sure your company's governance and operational policies are written down and disseminated to the firm's employees. As companies grow there is a tendency for more policies to be written down. Whatever the size of the organization, it's good to commit as many policies as possible to writing. Then those policies can be disseminated to the entire firm and over time behavior can come into congruence with those policies.

Policies can be both freeing and also limiting. A policy construct can provide guidance as to what is acceptable behavior, can describe who is responsible for various categories of decision-making and action, and save time and effort that may be wasted when managers have to think through a problem *ad hoc* each time the problem arises.

Also, policies can be limiting, but once they are written down they can be examined, refined, or eliminated. Many times, old policies hang around that are no longer relevant, or worse, constrain the business from needed action. Maybe the policy was good and effective at some point in the past and solved a problem back then. Now years have gone by, the problem no longer exists, but the policy is still around. Those kinds of policies need to be eradicated.

So, write your policies down and see what you have created for the firm. Do a review and get rid or modify the policies that hold you back. Always keep in mind the firm's strategic vision, and keep and use those policies that move the firm in the direction it needs to go.

Another important point. Employees need to know the policies, and the firm must be able to report accurately that it knows its employees know the firm's policies. It is good to have a regular schedule of training events at which the company instructs the employees about the firm's policies.

Learning from Failure

If a firm's failure is not fatal and the firm has recovered, the firm should study the failure and determine what went wrong. How, where and when did the responsible parties make the mistake? Was it in planning? Was the venture rolled out wrong? Was one of the "rights" violated: right place, right time, right price, and right quality? Was there an act of God that killed the venture? Did the government interfere? Answering these questions should lead to better decision-making downstream.

Now we move on to our case studies of failure. We hope you enjoy reading the cases, analyzing the questions, and learning from others' failures. Our hope is that you learn from the failures outlined in this book, and that you avoid these same failures going forward.

CHAPTER TWO

CASE STUDIES OF MANAGEMENT FAILURE

Large For-Profit Firms

and

Governmental Entities

This page intentionally left blank

Case 2.1: Amorous Relationship I

Problems with amorous relationships don't just happen in small companies, they also occur in *Fortune 500,* multi-billion-dollar companies. Consider the case of Henry Stonecipher, Chairman and CEO of The Boeing Company.

Stonecipher was born in 1936, and earned a bachelor's degree in physics from Tennessee Tech in 1960. He began work at Allison, then moved to GE's Large Engine Division in 1960. He was named a Vice President of GE in 1979, then in 1984 became a division head. He then moved to Sundstrand in 1987 and became CEO of Sundstrand in 1989. In 1994 Stonecipher was elected CEO of McDonnell Douglas where he worked on the merger with Boeing. He then became COO of McDonnell Douglas in its merged relationship with Boeing. He retired in 2002.

In 2003 Stonecipher was chosen to lead The Boeing Company after the ouster of Philip Condit as Boeing CEO. Condit had got caught up in several alleged scandals, one being a major contracting scandal with the U.S. Air Force, and one being accusations of affairs with Boeing employees.

Stonecipher had been the chairman at McDonnell Douglas. Stonecipher was given credit for the merger between Boeing and McDonnell Douglas. Stonecipher was given credit for turning Boeing around and getting it past the alleged Condit scandals. During his brief tenure as CEO of Boeing Stonecipher played a central role in the design and supply chain for the proposed new airplane, the B787, also known as the Dreamliner.

After just a short time as CEO, in 2005 Boeing's board requested Stonecipher's resignation. An investigation had found a consensual relationship with a Boeing executive, Debra Peabody. While there did not appear to be any special company benefits flowing to Peabody, the board decided it could not tolerate a breach of Boeing's code of conduct. Stonecipher's wife filed for divorce a few days after the affair was announced.

As reported by *Washington Post* staff writer Renae Merle on March 8, 2005:

> *It's not the fact that he was having an affair "that caused him to be fired," said Lewis E. Platt, Boeing's non-executive chairman. "But as we explored the circumstances surrounding the affair, we just thought there were some issues of poor judgment that...impaired his ability to lead going forward."*

Discussion Questions

1. After Condit's exit as CEO, should Boeing's Board have been more careful in selecting the next CEO?

2. What are some risks in hiring CEOs or other executive based on high-profile previous accomplishments?

3. Did the Board exercise its due diligence in chasing informal information about Stonecipher before appointing him as CEO?

4. What are some qualities a board should consider when considering a candidate for CEO?

5. What policies should Boeing have in place to attempt to head off amorous relationships between bosses and subordinates, or even between colleagues?

Analysis

It was obvious to Boeing's Board that Stonecipher was a brilliant leader. His track record at McDonald Douglas (MD) and his work in the Boeing-MD merger gave the Board much opportunity to see him at work. After Condit's exit with accusations of improper romantic alliances with subordinates, the Board should have been more attuned to behavior along those lines. Nevertheless, it went ahead with Stonecipher; he was able and he was available.

In the short time he was at Boeing he helped make the decision to move ahead with the Dreamliner, in spite of Airbus' decision to build the huge A380. Airline companies later justified Boeing's decision while the A380 languished.

Stonecipher's affair with a female VP began soon after he was appointed as CEO. An investigation revealed that she did not receive any special recognition or benefits from the relationship. She was not relieved of her job when Stonecipher was let go.

The Board chose brilliance over personal character. Even though Stonecipher did not violate any of Boeing's personnel policies, he did violate the Code of Values. His ability to lead was stained, and the Board eventually concluded he had to go.

Case 2.2: Daimler-Chrysler

Daimler-Benz and Chrysler merged in 1998 with a $36B buyout of Chrysler by Daimler-Benz. The new company was named DaimlerChrysler AG. The move was heralded in press releases as a merger of companies, but in reality, it turned out to be a takeover of Chrysler by Daimler.

There was logic in merging the two companies. By combining the two companies the new firm would have a complete line of automobiles from inexpensive cars for the new/young buyer to luxury cars for the wealthier. It was a repeat of the old General Motors approach of having five levels of cars through which a buyer could move as he or she moved through life: Chevrolet, Pontiac, Oldsmobile, Buick and Cadillac. The second major reason for this merger was the two firms could share car platforms and parts with a consequent reduction in costs. A third reason was the potential for rationalization of use of suppliers and assembly plants which would provide further cost reductions. A fourth reason was that Daimler wanted to sell more cars in North America and thought a tie would provide Daimler a stage for expansion of sales.

Before the merger the U.S. investor Kirk Kerkorian was trying to get control of Chrysler. Chrysler's head, Bob Eaton, did not want Kerkorian to take control, so he started merger discussions with Daimler's chief, Jergen Schrempp. It wasn't long after the merger before Schrempp forced Eaton into a secondary role, and Daimler was in control of the merged organization.

The merger never took hold. There was an immediate clash of cultures. According to an article in the *Harvard Business Review,* "…the two organizations really didn't like each other, and couldn't cooperate to the extent necessary to make the combination work. Serious efforts to integrate the operations of Daimler and Chrysler foundered on lack of trust clashes between the mid-market cowboys of Detroit and the high-end knights of Stuttgart."

Problems became evident when the good folks at the Mercedes-Benz sector did not want to share parts with Chrysler, because Chrysler was viewed as a mass-market company and Mercedes-Benz was viewed as a luxury firm.

Chrysler's sales dropped significantly soon after the merger, so Daimler appointed Dieter Zetsche to head the Chrysler sector. Zetsche led the Chrysler group in a return to profitability, then Zetsche went back to Germany to lead the parent company, which he headed until 2017.

Problems continued to boil between the two groups, so it was determined to break up the marriage. In May 2007 the Chrysler group was sold to the private equity firm Cerberus Capital Management for $7.4B, which gave Cerberus 80.1% of the firm, with Daimler retaining the other 19.9%. In October 2007 DaimlerChrysler AG changed its name to Daimler AG. In 2009 Daimler gave up its 19.9% share of the Chrysler group.

Discussion Questions

1. Why did the firms think it was important to report that the transition was a merger, rather than a takeover?

2. Was Chrysler's decision to go ahead with the merger just a quick reaction to Kerkorian's thrust?

3. What could Chrysler have done to prevent a takeover by Daimler?

4. What could the two firms have done to bring the two sets of employees together into one enterprise?

5. Did the merged firm give up too quickly when it spun off Chrysler?

Analysis

In hindsight, it is obvious that Daimler viewed bringing Daimler and Chrysler together was a takeover, not a merger. There was never any intent to give Chrysler people high positions in the newly merged group.

The cultures of the two companies were very different. The two sets of employees had different self-images about their companies; one group viewed itself as putting out high quality, high value automobiles, while the other set of employees thought of their product as middle-level in terms of quality and value. Neither side wanted to give up its base orientation.

The two sets of leaders did not adequately prepare for the merger. There should have been extensive education sessions concerning the merger. Leaders of both groups should have been brought together for planning sessions. Decisions about structure should have been made months before consummating the merger.

Senior management failed to get the two groups to cooperate with each other. Not sharing information and parts should have been nipped in the bud immediately.

Case 2.3: Hubris at the Top

It's not just modern managers who have made significant mistakes. History is replete with examples of leaders who made gross errors in judgment and wrecked their companies or wrecked their countries. Sometimes the problem comes from the hubris of the manager.

From Greek mythology we get the story of Oedipus Rex and his murders. From Shakespeare we have Hamlet. A figure closer to our times was Richard Nixon.

Nixon thought he was above the law. As Commander in Chief of the U.S. military he thought he could order the military to do anything he wanted. With respect to the civil authorities, he had control of the Department of Justice and thought he could evade the civil law. While attempting to keep his nefarious activities from the public, he recorded many of his conversations with subordinates; those recordings later got him into trouble.

As often happens, a particular incident brought Nixon down, and that was the break-in at the Democratic headquarters in the Watergate building in downtown Washington, D.C. Probably Nixon could have survived the bad publicity from that criminal activity, except for the cover-up Nixon tried to construct. The cover-up kept the story alive due to reporting in the *Washington Post* and other U.S. newspapers. Eventually the question of releasing the taped recordings went to the U.S. Supreme Court, where Nixon lost the right to keep the tapes secret. In time public opinion swayed against Nixon, and he resigned from the Presidency, the first and only President to do so.

Many who worked for Nixon found him to be a brilliant man, with wonderful abilities to develop strategies and tactics for taking the country forward. However, his brilliance led him astray, and he got ahead of good ethical practices. When found in sin, he attempted to cover it up, and that brought him down.

Discussion Questions

1. Why did Nixon feel he needed to cover up the Watergate caper, and particularly his involvement in the matter?

2. Is it wise for a leader to record his or her conversations with subordinates?

3. How can a leader with much power, such as one who is the head of a company, keep from developing arrogance and hubris?

4. Should managers admit mistakes and come clean right up front all the time?

5. Are there any cases where a manager should not admit they have made a mistake and keep quiet about it?

Analysis

As President of the United States, Nixon was arguably

the most powerful man in the world. He was head of the military, and head of the justice department. He had many tools at his disposal that could be used to make significant changes in the United States and in the rest of the world.

In 1972 he ran a campaign to get elected to a second term as President. Nixon was quite popular with the U.S. population, and the polls showed he was running well ahead of his opponent, George McGovern. Nevertheless, Nixon encouraged his team members to engage in illegal activity to try to gain even more leverage over the opposition.

Nixon had a big ego; he wanted to go down in history as a great President. He wanted his words to be known. He also seemed to be insecure. Because of these two dispositions, he decided to tape his conversations in the Oval Office. When the press got so close and it was discovered that he had taped conversations, a few allegedly significant minutes of the tape or tapes disappeared. The disappearance was viewed by many as his attempt to destroy incriminating evidence.

Case 2.4: Hubris Galore

One leader who was overcome by hubris was Adolph Hitler. He came to power in the 1930s in Germany after Germany was devastated by World War I and was in dire economic straits. By the force of his personality and willingness to use force and violence as management tools, he gained control of the government and brought prosperity back to the country. At the same time, he ran rough-shod over the rights of several minority groups.

He decided that Germany and Germans needed more room to flourish, so he sent the German armies east and west to conquer the neighboring countries. After conquering the nations around him, he determined he should go after the big German enemy to the east, the Union of Soviet Socialist Republics (USSR). In spite of having a non-aggression pact with Joseph Stalin, the leader of the USSR, in spite of warnings from his advisors, and in spite of the history of Napoleon's failure to conquer Russia, Hitler went ahead with project Barbarossa.

The German military initially met little resistance and moved far into USSR territory. With Hitler calling the shots, many times against the advice of his generals, Hitler did not take advantage of the army's gains as he sent divisions to the south to capture the oil fields of the Balkans. By the time the army was ready to move east again, winter set in, and the ill-equipped German army started to suffer the same fate that Napoleon's army had suffered 135 years earlier. The Russian winter was severe, and thousands of German soldiers froze to death.

The surge was halted, never to be regained. Barbarossa was a failure, and over half the German army on the East was killed, captured, or died from the cold.

Hitler still did not learn his lesson, and increasingly took charge of directing the actions of the army. This former corporal from World War I was countermanding the orders of his professional generals.

After Hitler made an enemy of Stalin and the USSR, the USSR armies started moving to the West, rolled up on Germany, and were at the gates of Berlin when Hitler finally conceded and committed suicide. Hitler was his own worst enemy.

Discussion Questions

1. Did Hitler need to use rough-shod tactics to become head of Germany?

2. Did the armistice conditions of WWI set up conditions for Hitler to come to power?

3. What should Hitler have learned from Napoleon's disaster in Russia?

4. Why was Hitler so anti-Semitic?

5. Would you consider Hitler a leader? Why or why not?

Analysis

The Allies who won WWI put conditions on Germany which made it impossible for the German economy to thrive. Living conditions deteriorated in Germany over the next decade and a half that made any savior look good. The German people bought into Hitler's rhetoric and overlooked the strong-arm tactics he used to gain control of country.

Hitler was a man of tremendous ego. He wanted to have tight control of all aspects of the economy, the military, and Germany's position in the world. He used his tools of power to put his stamp on the arts, education, the economy, science, and the military. He became, in effect, a dictator.

Although he was never an officer in the military, he viewed himself as superior to his generals, and often disregarded their advice. This got him into trouble after a couple of years of initial success. It took time for the opponent nations to wake up and start to build militaries that could counter Hitler's moves.

Hitler put lots of resources into the sciences and hoped that his military inventions would provide the winning solution to the problems the military eventually encountered. Those inventions were too little and too late to save Hitler's bacon.

Case 2.5: K-Mart

The first K-Mart store opened in 1962. Its corporate headquarters was located in Troy, Michigan, a suburb of Detroit. K-Mart, a derivative of the S.S. Kresge Five and Dime stores, was a big box department store which competed with such companies as Hills, Zayre, and Ames. Over time it operated under various names and had several subsidiaries, such as Borders Books, KDollar, Office Max, Payless Drugs, Kmart Super Center, Big Mart, Kmart Express, Kmart Dental, American Fare, and The Sports Authority. K-Mart bought and sold various subsidiaries over the years as it expanded and contracted its scope of sales. In some years K-Mart used the name Kmart.

K-Mart was started the same year Walmart was incorporated, 1962. For the first 25 years K-Mart led Walmart in sales and number of stores. At the 25-year mark, 1987, K-Mart had twice as many stores as Walmart. By the year 2000, K-Mart had over 2000 stores and over 100 Kmart Super Center locations. The turn of the century was the high-water mark for K-Mart. By 2005 the corporation had closed over 500 of its stores and over 50 of its Super Centers.

In the meantime, K-Mart's store properties were becoming dated. Many shoppers found the aisles narrow and difficult to maneuver. Many of the properties didn't look good and were in disrepair. The K-Mart Board and several successive CEOs tried varies strategies to improve sales, most without good effect.

In 2002 the firm filed for bankruptcy. In 2003 alone

K-Mart lost over 300 stores. K-Mart got out of bankruptcy in 2003 and took on a new name: K-Mart Holding Corporation. In 2004 K-Mart purchased Sears and put Sears and the K-Mart assets under the name Sears Holding Corporation. The Sears Holding Corporation headquarters was placed in Illinois.

K-Mart and Sears continued to decline. More stores in the two divisions were closed after the merger, and there was speculation whether Sears would be able to survive. By the end of 2017 there were slightly more than 500 K-Mart stores left and one Super Center. In 2017, for the first time in recent years, Sears and K-Mart did not put out any television advertisements during the Christmas holidays. By 2018 K-Mart had closed all its stores outside the United States and Puerto Rico.

In October 2018, Sears Holdings declared Chapter 11 bankruptcy and announced plans to close 142 unprofitable stores. In August 2018, sears Holding announced closings of 46 stores. As of the date of this writing Sears Holding had 687 stores remaining.

Discussion Questions

1. Should a retail company such as K-Mart change its strategy every time a new CEO comes on board?

2. Did K-Mart expand too fast?

3. Why did Walmart succeed but K-Mart fail?

4. Why didn't K-Mart keep up its properties?

5. Should K-Mart have bought Sears, or should Sears have bought K-Mart? What difference does it make?

Analysis

K-Mart started out in a good position; it had the experience of the Kresge company behind it. It grew quickly; some might say it grew too fast. It brought a new shopping experience to the customer in bright new buildings.

Over time K-Mart let its buildings deteriorate. Aisles were crowded; too much merchandise was put on the floor. Over time K-Mart came to be known for lower quality products, except for the name brands K-Mart carried.

K-Mart was not known for its supply chain management system, which was one matter in which Walmart excelled. Supply chain management was not a competitive advantage for K-Mart.

K-Mart faced very strong competition from Walmart and similar big box stores. It always appeared to be playing catch-up.

Eventually K-Mart bought out Sears, another retail giant whose glory days had already past. Some said it was for the purpose of getting hold of the properties, not for real interest in the retail business. After the buy-out the two groups continued to be run principally as two separate groups; there didn't appear to be interest in synergy between the two.

Case 2.6: Montgomery Ward

Aaron Montgomery Ward was a dry-goods salesman who worked in the upper Midwest after the Civil War. In his sales work he observed that many of his customers did not have access to goods that were available in the larger cities, so in 1872 Ward and some partners developed a catalog. The partners soon left, but Ward's catalog business grew quite rapidly and within ten years the catalog had over 200 pages. By the turn of the century Ward was mailing out nearly three million catalogs. The company was named Montgomery Ward. Ward built several distribution centers, first in Chicago, and then around the country.

Montgomery Ward opened its first retail store in 1926, in Indiana. Within three years it had more than 500 retail outlet stores. The firm lost money during the depression, but turned down an offer to merge with its principal rival, Sears Roebuck & Co. In 1930 the firm hired Sewell Avery, formerly President of U. S. Gypsum, as president of the company; the firm soon returned to profitability under Avery's leadership.

In 1944 Avery and Montgomery Ward got into trouble with the Federal government. Ward employees went on strike, and Avery refused to settle the strike. President Roosevelt, using his wartime powers, seized all of Montgomery Ward's property in the United States. When Roosevelt died and Truman became President, Truman restored the property to Montgomery Ward.

Avery was still president after the close of WWII.

He thought the country would enter a depression. He wanted to save as much money as he could so he would be able to buy up the competition. He didn't buy or open up new stores nor spruce up the old ones. In the meantime, Sears Roebuck & Co. was aggressively enlarging, as were competitors like J.C. Penney, Gimbels and Macys. Avery continued to hold the president's position until 1954.

In the early 1960s Montgomery Ward's catalog sales started to decline. Also, a succession of CEOs led the charge to reduce costs and increase the use of private brands. In 1968 Montgomery Ward merged with Container Corporation of America; the new name for the holding company was MARCOR. In 1973 the firm bought Jefferson Stores, a discount chain based in Miami. Those stores were renamed as Jefferson Ward stores. MARCOR was bought out by Mobil Oil in 1974. In 1985 the company closed down its catalog operations. In 1988 company management took Montgomery Ward private in a leveraged buyout.

In the late 1980s the company started into the electronics business. It was one of the first retail firms to sell electronics items from Sony, Panasonic, Hewlett Packard, Apple, and Compaq. It dedicated space in its stores to a SOHO (Small Office Home Office) department and ran a very successful campaign selling PCs to small businesses and students. In the early 1990s it re-entered the catalog market, but just for a short time.

In 1997 the firm filed for bankruptcy. It got out of bankruptcy in 1999, but was now owned by GE Capital.

The firm was renamed as Wards. In late December 2000 the firm began to close down, and began to liquidate its assets. By May 2001 it was gone.

Discussion Questions

1. Speculate as to the work of the board during the time of Avery's leadership.
2. Why did Avery think there would be a depression after WWII?
3. Discuss how changing leadership and strategies can harm or help a company.
4. Why was Montgomery Ward passed around by several companies?
5. What are some key aspects of managing a large store chain such as Montgomery Ward?

Analysis

The failure of Montgomery Ward might be attributed to one man, Sewell Avery. After a brilliant career turning Montgomery Ward around in the 1930s, and working for the government during WWII, Avery continued as President of Montgomery Ward until 1954. Altogether, Avery was President from 1930 until 1954. His futurist prediction after WWII was that the country would move into a depression, so he did not expand the company, and let the properties deteriorate. At the same time Sears Roebuck & Co. was aggressively expanding. Montgomery Ward never did recover its competitive position.

The company kept changing its strategies. Each CEO seemed to have a different approach as to increasing sales; most didn't work. Montgomery Ward was then passed around by several companies which had ownership; that didn't lead to consistent leadership and strategy. Finally, Montgomery Ward couldn't keep its catalog sales going – a key feature of its early success.

Case 2.7: Bernie Madoff

This is the case of Bernard (Bernie) Madoff, who died in 2021 while serving a 150-year sentence for the work he did leading a Ponzi scheme that lost an estimated $40B for its clients. This has been alleged to be the largest fraud case in the history of U.S. finance.

Madoff was born in New York in 1938. His father ran a sporting goods store, which he lost during the Korean War. Madoff attended the University of Alabama for one year, then transferred to Hofstra University where he majored in political science and graduated in 1960.

Madoff started his first company at age 22, the Bernard L. Madoff Investment Securities LLC. By the late 1980s Madoff was making an estimated $100M a year. He became chairman of NASDAQ in 1990 and served three one-year terms in the 1990s.

Madoff's Ponzi scheme began in 1991, he later reported. He claimed to be able to return exceptionally high percentages on investments. When a client wanted his or her money back, Madoff often wasn't able to produce it from existing funds, so he would solicit and get more investors and use the new investment money to pay off the old clients who wanted out.

Madoff had a personality that led people to trust him. He particularly led Jewish investors to participate with him. Especially hurt in the final disposition of the fund were the Elie Wiesel Foundation for Peace and the Hadassah charity.

One of Madoff's early detractors was Harry Markopolos, the financial fraud investigator, who filed various complaints with the Securities and Exchange Commission over the years. The SEC apparently didn't follow up on the complaints.

In 2008 Madoff confessed his problems to his sons; the sons turned him in soon thereafter. Eventually Madoff was accused and tried for several felonies. In 2009 he pleaded guilty to 11 of the counts. In June 2009 Madoff was sentenced to 150 years in prison and was forced to give up $170M of his assets. At the time Madoff's firm closed it stated its assets as worth $64B.

Madoff's two sons died after he went to prison. His son Mark committed suicide in 2010 and son Andrew died of cancer in 2014.

In 2017, the Department of Justice began to reimburse victims of Madoff's criminal behavior. The amount was announced as $772M to be divided among Madoff's 24,000 victims.

Madoff served his time in the Federal Correctional Complex in Butner, North Carolina. A July 18, 2019 article in the *Wall Street Journal* reported that "One of the largest offshore fund managers that channeled cash to Bernard Madoff will return $860 million in stolen money under a settlement with the liquidators cleaning up after the Ponzi scheme." (Scurria, *Wall Street Journal,* Page B3)

After Madoff went to prison HBO developed a film about Madoff's life and his Ponzi scheme. It is titled

"Wizard of Lies."

Discussion Questions

1. Should Madoff's sons have known something was wrong with the company even before he confessed?

2. Why did the SEC not investigate the complaints about Madoff's operation?

3. Does the SEC have any accountability for not investigating complaints that were filed?

4. Should the Federal government have a system in place to reimburse victims for financial crimes such as Madoff's?

5. Madoff served three terms as head of NASDAQ. How can a firm like NASDAQ protect itself from selecting leaders who have a pleasing personality but are unethical in their business practices?

Analysis

The SEC failed in its duties to investigate complaints about the Madoff operation. There were repeated complaints, but no follow-through. Madoff continued his nefarious practices even though he knew he was doing wrong to his clients.

Madoff took advantage of his religious connections, gaining many investors from the Jewish community and hurting two significant Jewish organizations, the Wiesel

Foundation for Peace and the Hadassah charity.

Madoff's sons had more integrity than Madoff. After they discovered what was going on they turned in their own father to the authorities. One wonders if the sons had some inkling of the illegal activities years before turning in their father.

The ones who suffered were the victim investors. They were fortunate if they recovered fifty cents on the dollar.

CHAPTER THREE

CASE STUDIES OF MANAGEMENT FAILURE

Small For-Profit Firms

This page intentionally left blank

Case 3.1: Be Careful with Email

Joe Wilson was the manager of the human resource department at XYZ Liquidators. Wilson was having issues with one of his employees, Rachelle Neto, whose performance had steadily decreased over the past several months. Neto called in sick at least a couple of times per month. Wilson addressed the issue with Neto, who explained that she was going through a tough time personally. Neto's poor attendance had placed a strain on the human resource office, and some of the other employees had to pick up the slack. Wilson frequently vented to one of his other employees, Samantha Jenkins, who often had to pick up the slack for Neto when she missed work.

One Monday morning Wilson came into his office and noticed he had a voice mail. The message was from Neto, who indicated that she had to take care of some personal issues that day, and that she would not be coming to work. Wilson slammed the phone down after listening to the message, and sighed, as he knew that Jenkins was not going to be happy about covering for Neto yet again. Wilson logged on to his computer and opened his email, where he began to compose a message to Jenkins letting her know that Neto was going to be absent that day. The message read:

Good morning Samantha,

You are not going to believe it, but Rachelle just called in sick AGAIN. I am sick and tired of this! She is such a flake, and her attendance is getting worse. When she is here, the environment is so tense because everyone can tell she has problems. I wish she would just quit. Let me know if you need any help today picking up the slack for our slacker!

Joe

After drafting the message, Wilson realized he did not complete the header. While Neto was heavy on his mind, Wilson started to type "Rach" into the "To" field, and the field self-populated with "Rachelle Neto." In the "Subject" field, Wilson entered "Here we go again." Without a second thought, Wilson clicked the Send button, and the standard confirmation box appeared across Wilson's computer screen: "Your message to Rachelle Neto has been sent."

Wilson just about fell out of his chair when he realized his mistake. Instead of sending the email about Neto to Jenkins, he accidentally sent it to Neto herself. Wilson immediately began to contemplate how he was going to talk his way out of this one.

Discussion Questions

1. How could Wilson have handled the downturn in Neto's performance?

2. How could Wilson have handled Neto's excessive absences?

3. Should Wilson be venting to staff about other staff members?

4. What are some ways managers can avoid these types of mistakes when sending e-mails?

5. Is there anything Jenkins could have done to keep from having to do Neto's work when Neto was gone?

Analysis

The story doesn't give us all the information we need about XYZ Liquidators. Let's begin by talking about policies that should be in place. First, there should be sick-leave policies that give boundary conditions on sick days and sick pay. There should be teeth in the policy to permit a termination if the privilege is abused. There should be disability insurance coverage for long-term disability. The policy should, of course, cover instances of illness protected by law.

Wilson should be monitoring Neto's performance. There should be contemporaneous records kept of incidents of poor performance. At least once a month there should be an evaluation of Neto's performance and a conversation with Neto giving her an update on expectations and her performance vis-à-vis the expectations. There should be a progressive discipline process that Wilson should be applying consistently.

Wilson allowed himself to get out of control by writing the letter to Jenkins. He shouldn't have been discussing Neto's performance with Jenkins; Neto's fulfillment of her performance expectations should be kept between Neto and Wilson. Further, Wilson wrote when he was angry and was not careful in putting in the address.

Wilson should not be telling one employee that another employee should quit. That is typically confidential information between the employee and that employee's supervisor. Managers must be careful to maintain professionalism all the time – even when frustration is overwhelming.

Case 3.2: Remote Termination

Better Mortgage, also known as Better.com, is a New York City based firm that lends money in several categories, especially for home purchases. It also offers "insurance and other services for home buyers." Better has approximately 10,000 employees. The following statement is taken from its website:

Better Mortgage is an Equal Housing Lender. As prohibited by federal law, we do not engage in business practices that discriminate on the basis of race, color, religion, national origin, sex, marital status, age (provided you have the capacity to enter into a binding contract), because all or part of your income may be derived from any public assistance program, or because you have, in good faith, exercised any right under the Consumer Credit Protection Act. The federal agency that administers our compliance with these federal laws is the Federal Trade Commission, Equal Credit Opportunity, Washington, DC, 20580.

Better Mortgage may be contacted as follows:

Better Mortgage Corporation

3 World Trade Center, 175 Greenwich Street, 59th Floor
New York, NY 10007
415-523-8837
Fax: 408-946-0112
NMLS # 330511
www.nmlsconsumeraccess.org

The current CEO of Better is Vishal Garg. In 2021 Garg determined that Better should be leaner and decided to engage in a drastic downsizing initiative. To do so, he identified 900 employees that would be let go. However, the thought of holding 900 one-on-one meetings with affected employees to let them know they were no longer going to work for the company seemed daunting, so he came up with another solution.

Garg arranged a videoconference via Zoom in December 2021, and invited the 900 employees to attend. It was then that Garg told everyone "If you're on this call, you are part of the unlucky group that is being laid off." He proceeded to let them know that "Your employment here is terminated effective immediately" (Maruf, 2021). The 900 employees represented 9% of the firm's employees.

As reported by the *Wall Street Journal* on January 20, 2022, Better Mortgage's board suspended Garg from his CEO duties shortly thereafter, and "hired an outside firm to assess its culture and leadership." Garg was reinstated to his role as CEO in January 2022 after reflecting on his leadership and working with an executive coach. The board reported that "We are confident in Vishal and in the changes he is committed to making to provide the type of leadership, focus, and vision that Better needs at this pivotal time" (*Wall Street Journal*, p. B-2)

"Mr. Garg apologized again …in a separate letter to employees, saying that he is sorry for the distraction and embarrassment his actions caused. He said he would be more conscious of the impact his words have on people."

Discussion Questions

1. Why did Vishal Garg separate the 900 employees over Zoom?

2. What other ways can a company effectively execute a massive layoff like this?

3. Should the CEO of a company be the one to notify employees of their separation from the company?

4. How can a company separate a good employee with dignity and grace?

5. What else should be considered when an employee must be let go?

Analysis

The story leaves much information out about the separation of 900 employees at once. We need to know what analysis was done to conclude that 900 employees (almost 10% of the company's employees) needed to go. Was the Board involved in that decision? How about the HR department? What about department managers?

The use of a mass virtual meeting to let a person know that he or she is being separated from the company is not a good way to treat employees, even if they are leaving the company. Apparently, there was no advance notice, no build-up, so the employees would know what was going to happen. They were blindsided.

Garg did not need to make the announcement himself. Once the decision was made as to which employees should go, the announcement to the employees could have been done in person by the employee's department manager.

We have no information as to whether there was a financial or other type of parachute for the departing employees. The blow could have been softened by some type of severance package.

Case 3.3: Don't Burn Your Bridges

George Williamson was the office manager of a service firm in Arkansas. The firm had sales of $200M each year. Profits were typically in the 10% range after taxes and interest. The firm had 175 employees. The average salary for the non-executive employees was $68,000. Williamson was considered to be part of the executive team and made a salary of $125,000 each year. Williamson reported directly to the CEO. The CEO had a compensation package that averaged $800,000 a year.

The firm was growing at the rate of about 15% a year and next year planned to add another 20 employees, including eight more to the office staff. The CEO determined that when the additional workers were added to the office staff, the work of the office should be reorganized into two divisions and another office manager should be added.

Sure enough, the additional staff were added, and a second office manager was added at a level comparable to Williamson. Williamson's value to the firm was recognized by a 20% salary increase. The new office manager's salary was pegged close to Williamson's. While Williamson's work was refocused, he no longer had total responsibility for the office.

Williamson felt diminished in his new role. He did not have oversight of all the office employees. He had to share some reporting time to the CEO and concluded he was left out of some decisions and information flow he previously had enjoyed. As time went on he became disgruntled and his attitude changed. He got into arguments with his subordinates. A couple of times he got into arguments with clients.

After six months of this arrangement Williamson decided he had enough. He was mad that he was no longer the kingpin in the office. He was mad at his diminished work with the CEO. He was mad at the entire firm. So, one Thursday he marched into the CEO's office and put a resignation letter on the CEO's desk, effective at the end of the next day.

The CEO read the letter and was very surprised. He talked to Williamson and told Williamson how valuable he was to the firm and everything was going well. Williamson didn't need to go; he was asked to stay. Williamson boiled over, told the CEO off, and refused to stay. He stomped out of the CEO's office, went to his own office, and started to pack.

The next day, Friday, Williamson's last day, the CEO organized a quick going-away party for Williamson. Williamson came to the party, but clearly wasn't enjoying it. At 4:00pm Williamson took his last box down to his car. At 5:00pm he dropped his keys on the CEO's desk, said goodbye, and left the building.

Monday morning the office staff came to work as usual and logged on to their computers. They found that none of their passwords worked. They determined that Williamson had changed the access codes to all employees' accounts and to all clients' data files. It took a week for IT to restore access to everyone and for business to resume.

Williamson, in the meantime, was out looking for work. Six weeks after quitting he wrote an e-mail to the CEO asking for a letter of recommendation. The CEO refused.

Discussion Questions

1. What policies should the company have instituted regarding password control?
2. What protocols should the company have put in place regarding employees exiting the firm?
3. What could Williamson have done to alleviate the problem that caused him such grief?
4. What signs can managers look out for to spot a disgruntled employee?
5. Should the CEO have refused to give a letter of recommendation to Williamson?

Analysis

Within a period of six months, George Williamson went from being a productive, friendly, and supportive manager to a disgruntled employee. The firm lost a useful employee who had potential to assist the firm for several more years.

Several things happened that caused the change and Williamson's decision to leave the firm. First, the CEO did not spend enough time working with Williamson and preparing Williamson for the changes that were coming. There was opportunity to talk about the growth of the company, how profits were improving, and how important

Williamson was to the firm's success. The CEO could have kept Williamson more informed about the CEO's thinking and direction and how the work would be even more stimulating than before.

Williamson should have been on the team that interviewed the applicants for the other office manager position. Williamson should have been part of the group that chose the new head. Also, after the new office manager was hired, the CEO should have included both managers in discussions to make sure they were on the same page and working well together.

On the company's part, there should have been in place protocols for normal password control. There should have also been special procedures and protocols to work with exiting employees to protect password access and company files.

Finally, Williamson must share a great deal of the blame for his own disgruntlement. Williamson had a good thing going; he was part of a dynamic company, had status in that company, and his compensation was not going to be diminished with the new structure. Apparently, he was insecure in his position. It was highly unethical for Williamson to change the passwords as he left the firm. Added to his discontented personality the last few weeks he was with the firm, the password caper left a bad taste in the mouths of the CEO and Williamson's colleagues.

Case 3.4: Choose Your Lawyer Carefully

Plains Training, Inc. was a firm based in Tulsa that provided training programs for the health industry in the six-state area of Oklahoma, Texas, Kansas, Louisiana, Arkansas, and Missouri. The firm provided seminars and workshops for hospitals, clinics, and small-businesses on such topics as legal and risk mitigation, cybersecurity, and individual coaching. Annual gross revenues were $35M; clean profit was approximately 10% of gross revenues. The company was growing at about 10% a year. Plains was a closely-held corporation owned by three investors. The CEO was Jeffrey Coates, who had been the CEO for five years.

As Coates travelled around the region he noticed that many of the smaller cities and towns through which he passed had financial trouble. There were bankruptcies, failed bond issues, infrastructure problems, and school funding difficulties. Coates thought he could help those cities by extending Plains' services to include seminars and workshops for cities, towns, and Chambers of Commerce.

At an industry conference Coates came across City Training, a firm based in Little Rock that provided help for cities and towns in a region that overlapped Plains' region. It was very much a smaller version of Plains. City's annual revenues were running around $10M and clean profits had been 7% of gross revenues for the past three years. After Coates studied City for five months he decided to see if Plains could buy City. Coates got a go-ahead nod from Plains' three owners, and started a courtship with City.

Coates started to develop a relationship with City's management team. After five months of discussions Coates made an offer to buy City. Discussions went well and a draft contract was worked out by Coates and the CEO of City.

At this stage Coates determined that the lawyers should get involved. He had run into a national-class lawyer at several industry conferences who was highly knowledgeable about the seminar and training industry. Coates proposed to the owners that this particular lawyer be retained to advise Plains about the proposed buy-out of City. The owners demurred because of that lawyer's high fees, so Coates had to go to Plains' usual legal group there in Tulsa.

Now Plains' legal work was done by a Tulsa firm that was on an annual retainer. It was a general legal office that provided normal legal advice to its client firms. Unfortunately, it had no experience in the seminar and workshop training industry, and had little experience in firm purchases of the type Plains was proposing. Plains' contact lawyer at the firm studied the proposed contract and concluded it was a bad deal for Plains. The conditions were too onerous. The price was too high. Plains would be betting the company. The lawyer made such a stink about the proposed purchase that Coates and his owners backed off the purchase. Coates continued to talk with City's management, but as the months wore on City's folks got disgusted with the pace of the negotiations and closed down discussions.

Five months later City was bought by National Trainers, Inc., an Indianapolis-based training firm. National moved aggressively to serve cities in Plains' region, and Plains was closed off from that market.

Discussion Questions

1. When should a firm have an in-house counsel?

2. When is it better to put a single-person law firm on retainer? When is it better to have on retainer one of the bigger state or national law firms with many lawyers?

3. How would you determine if the lawyer you are working with has knowledge/experience dealing with your type of legal problem?

4. When do you need to follow the advice of your attorney? When might you reject that advice?

5. As a manager, how do you know at what point a lawyer should be consulted?

Analysis

There are several ways to go about securing legal counsel. Some firms hire a lawyer full time to represent the firm in legal matters, thus creating an in-house attorney's office. Other firms will retain a single outside lawyer to represent the firm. Still other firms will retain a local legal office where there is a bevy of lawyers. Then some firms will retain a national or global legal corporation, with offices in many cities around the globe, to represent its interests.

When a firm has a legal problem to resolve, there is always the question of which attorney to use to resolve the question at hand. Does the firm need a generalist or a specialist? Of course, the need has to be balanced with the costs, because national-class legal experts may charge a few thousand dollars per hour for their services. However, if the situation is critical enough, it may pay to get the very best counsel available.

Not all lawyers are created equal. Just because a person has been to law school and has a Juris Doctor (J.D.) degree does not guarantee that lawyer will know all that much about your problem. At the least, the firm must find an attorney who has experience with your kind of problem, knows the laws dealing with that situation, and is familiar with matters that are to be covered in contracts dealing with your situation.

Coates, representing Plains Training, did not push enough against his own investors and his regular legal firm. Coates eventually settled for a mediocre attorney who didn't know much about the training business. He didn't know the field, and didn't know the pitfalls that get in the way of success of training firms. He couldn't get ahead of the game, didn't know what standard practice was, and didn't know good advice to give to Plains. After too much time has passed, Plains was left high and dry.

Case 3.5: Safety First

ABC Auto is a company that distributes auto parts to various auto dealers and auto parts retail stores. Their 30,000 square foot warehouse consists of rows of industrial shelving on which pallets of materials are stored. Some of these shelves are over 15 feet high. Once an order is received, the order is assigned to an employee, who then pulls the merchandise, prepares it for shipment, and creates an invoice.

Johnny Silva has worked in the warehouse at ABC Auto for six years. One day as he was assigned an order, Silva jumped on the forklift and began pulling the order. As he drove to shelving unit 45C, Silva proceeded to remove a pallet containing a rebuilt car engine from the middle shelf. In doing so, he noticed a small crack in the main shelving's vertical support beam. After a brief inspection, Silva returned to pulling the order. Once he fulfilled the order and it was invoiced, Silva went on a break. On his way to the break room, he stopped by the office of Manny Ramirez, the warehouse manager. He reported the small crack in shelf 45C to Ramirez. Ramirez was busy preparing for a corporate audit that was scheduled to take place first thing the next morning. Ramirez asked Silva how big the crack was, and he explained it was small, approximately two inches long, and not very wide. Silva described it as a "hairline crack." Ramirez told Silva he would look at it later, so Silva proceeded to the break room to take his break.

The next morning the corporate inspection began. Three representatives from the corporate office visited the warehouse. Two representatives were responsible for surveying the office records and paperwork, and the third representative, Tommy John, was responsible for conducting a safety inspection on the warehouse including its fixtures and equipment. During the course of the warehouse safety inspection, John interviewed several warehouse personnel, including Silva. John asked Silva if he was aware of any safety issues or concerns related to the warehouse. Silva mentioned that he had reported a crack in the shelving unit to the warehouse manager the previous day, and took John over to shelving unit 45C to show him the crack. John inspected the shelving unit, took some notes, and thanked Silva for his time. John continued the inspection of the warehouse.

Upon completion of the inspection that afternoon, the three corporate representatives met with Ramirez to debrief and review any issues or concerns. In addition to the representatives sharing several concerns with invoicing and backup documentation of certain orders, John reported the issue of the crack in shelving unit 45C. John indicated that the shelving unit needed to be immediately decommissioned and disposed of properly. Ramirez ensured he would have the warehouse personnel get on it immediately. The corporate representatives left the warehouse.

Ramirez began to make lists of all of the adjustments he needed to make in the office with regard to policies, procedures, and recordkeeping. He was scheduled to go on vacation the following week, so his level of urgency to get the office cleaned up was high. Later that afternoon Silva visited Ramirez's office to let him know that John had inspected the cracked shelving unit earlier that morning. Ramirez indicated that he knew, and that he would have to deal with that later because he had to get the office cleaned up before his vacation. Silva returned to work and went about his business.

The next morning, as Silva was pulling an order, he needed to retrieve a pallet of merchandise from shelf 45C. In doing so, Silva noticed that the crack had gotten larger – it had about doubled in size from before. After pulling the order, Silva reported the increase in the size of the crack to Ramirez. Ramirez's response was "I don't have time to deal with that right now. We will look at it when I get back from vacation!" Silva returned to work.

The following week while Ramirez was on vacation, a large order of parts came in that needed to be put away in the warehouse. Silva was assigned to put the merchandise away. One item was a rebuilt car engine, which was to be stored on shelf 45C. As Silva was using the forklift to place the heavy pallet on the shelving unit, the shelf broke, and it came crashing down on the forklift along with all of the merchandise that was stored on the shelf. In a knee-jerk reaction, Silva bailed from the forklift; several of the pallets fell on top of him, severely injuring him.

Discussion Questions

1. Did Silva do anything wrong in reporting the broken shelving?

2. How could Ramirez have kept track of the work he needed to do to take care of the cracked shelf?

3. While waiting for the shelf to be repaired, what should Ramirez have done?

4. Is the company responsible for the Silva's medical bills after his injury?

5. How does a manager determine the severity of a safety issue in the workplace?

Analysis

Ramirez made a major mistake by not taking care of the broken shelving unit immediately. It created a dangerous situation, and did indeed cause Silva's serious injury. Ramirez should have repaired the shelf as soon as the crack was reported to him. Least of all, he should have taken that shelf out of service until it could be repaired.

This leads to the question about the other shelving. How often are the shelves inspected for cracks and breaks? Are the inspections documented and records kept?

In order to protect himself, Silva should have kept contemporaneous records of his notice to Ramirez. This would help absolve him in case there was an argument later about who notified whom and when.

The representatives from corporate also needed a tracking system to assure a follow-up on repairing the cracked shelf. Rather than just drawing the matter to Ramirez' attention, the assurance that the repair had been made should have been indicated in the records.

It is easy for a manager to get busy with activities that are urgent and forget ones that do not appear to be critical. The manager needs to have a system for keeping track of activities that need to be done, a system that would not let him or her forget needed work.

Case 3.6: Fooling Around

Bill Rathbone was Vice President for Sales of a $50M firm on the East Coast. Rathbone was an all-around good guy, an excellent leader, and a person well loved by his peers and superiors. He was a handsome man, athletic, an excellent conversationalist, and a great storyteller.

Rathbone's division of the firm was doing quite well. The firm's sales were growing at a rate of about 10% per year. Rathbone kept in close touch with the head of production, and the production side of the firm was in sync with sales, so customers were getting their goods on time, and with high quality. In the firm Rathbone was given credit for the coordinated efforts of sales and production.

Rathbone was in his early forties. He was married to a beautiful woman, who was an outstanding real-estate salesperson. The Rathbones had two boys, both in high school. The boys were good students and excelled in high-school athletics. The Rathbones lived in a 5500 square-foot mansion with six bedrooms, four baths, a swimming pool, and a 4-car garage, all overlooking the scenic Hudson River.

At the office Rathbone worked closely with his assistant, Louise Wilson. Wilson was a college graduate with a major in English. Rathbone trusted her explicitly. When Rathbone wanted to write a business letter he would often tell Wilson what he wanted, then Wilson would write the letter and send it off without Rathbone looking at it. Wilson kept Rathbone's calendar of appointments. She would often help Rathbone by buying birthday and Christmas gifts for Rathbone's family members. On days when Rathbone did not have a business luncheon Rathbone and Wilson would often go to lunch together. The lunches tended to be, as they were named in the firm, two-martini lunches.

As the months wore on it was obvious to Rathbone's co-workers that Rathbone and Wilson were becoming more than business colleagues. Rathbone's spoken references to Wilson were on a familiar basis, and it was quite clear that he admired and liked her. One of the colleagues discovered that they had gone to a conference together in Cancún. This was repeated two months later at a conference in San Diego.

Within a six months period the relationship had turned romantic. Rathbone and Wilson would disappear from the office for long lunches, sometimes as long as three hours. After lunch they would go to a local hotel and carry on their romantic trysts.

The office staff suspected what was going on, and one person reported it to the CEO. The CEO brushed the report aside. He couldn't believe that Rathbone, with all that Rathbone had going for himself, would get involved romantically with his assistant. As far as the CEO was concerned, Rathbone was always Johnny-on-the-spot, was still doing a good job, and it was just jealous colleagues who thought something nefarious was going on.

The affair between Rathbone and Wilson

progressed with the two spending more time together. Eventually Rathbone's wife figured out that something was changing in their marriage relationship and started to sniff out the problem. She accused Rathbone of the affair, which he denied. After a couple of more months, Rathbone's wife called the CEO and reported what was going on.

After the wife's report, the CEO finally decided he needed to investigate the situation. He started nosing around and discovered that the rumor mill in Rathbone's division was rife with accusations of the affair. Several thought Wilson was getting undeserved perks. Morale was low in the division.

After consulting with the firm's attorney and the head of HR, the CEO knew he had to act. Further, he determined that things had gotten so bad in the division that Rathbone had to go. He called Rathbone in for a meeting and gave Rathbone his walking papers. He did give Rathbone a good severance package, and Rathbone was out the door immediately. Rathbone's access to the firm's computers was shut down and Rathbone was asked to leave his office that same day.

Discussion Questions

1. When a supervisor hears a rumor or suspects that a subordinate is doing something illegal, immoral, or unwise, how soon should the supervisor confront the issue?

2. When hearing a rumor about a subordinate's behavior, should the supervisor ask for the

accusation in writing before acting?

3. If a subordinate reports illegal or immoral activity of another worker, should the accused worker be able to confront the accuser?

4. When should a supervisor bring the HR office into a discussion about a subordinate's inappropriate behavior?

5. What steps can an employee take to make sure he or she does not get into a tempting situation that would lead to illegal or immoral behavior?

Analysis

Here's another management failure. Rathbone failed by starting an affair with his assistant. He knew better, but one thing led to another and he fell into the trap of turning a business connection into a romantic relationship. The CEO failed by letting the romantic relationship go so long before investigating the report.

If he had acted immediately, he might have been able to counsel Rathbone in a way that would have saved Rathbone for the company, restored morale in the division, and kept the firm on track. By not acting he had to replace a senior leader in the firm, which took much of the CEO's time, cost nearly $150,000, and took several months of search time with loss of momentum and morale.

Case 3.7: Don't Settle Too Quickly

Rapco Steel was a medium size conglomerate based in Philco, Alabama. Jameson Construction was a wholly owned subsidiary of Rapco, with annual sales of $30M, and net annual profits of $5M. Jameson's accumulated reserves at the time of the action described below totaled $750,000, while Rapco's reserves were $3.5M. George Harrington was CEO of Jameson.

Rachel Walters was a former employee of Jameson; she had been away from the company for two years. Walters instituted a claim against Jameson in which she accused Harrington of sexual assault. Walters' attorneys asked for a settlement for $3M. Walters' attorneys reported they would be willing to sign a nondisclosure agreement.

The claim was first considered by Jameson's HR department. After investigation, the HR department found that the claimant, Walters, had a significant case against Harrington, and some kind of settlement should be made. Given the amount of money involved, the matter was kicked upstairs to Rapco and Rapco's attorneys, who were brought into the case. Rapco's attorneys met with Walters' attorneys to determine for themselves if Walters had a good case. Rapco was convinced that Walters had a case, but Rapco thought they might be able to beat the case in court.

Internal to Rapco, the lawyers decided what move to make. One option would be to offer Walters a smaller amount of money. They first made an offer of $100,000, which Walters refused. Then they tried

$300,000, which Walters also refused. Walters' attorneys let the Rapco attorneys know that Walters was adamant and would accept only the full $3M. Then Rapco's attorneys asked themselves whether they should just let the case go to trial. If they went to trial then the firm's reputation would be hurt. In addition, they estimated that total court cost would be about $1.4M. There was not total agreement among the lawyers; some argued for the court case and believed the hit on Rapco's reputation would be short-lived. After much discussion and internal discord, Rapco agreed that Rapco would pay the full $3M with a signed nondisclosure agreement. In the meantime, Harrington was fired. Walters went away feeling justified with a fat pocketbook, while most of Rapco's reserves were wiped out.

Fifteen months later a Jameson employee, Martha Blonn, came forward with a sexual harassment claim against Harrington. In her claim she noted that Walters had filed such a claim and had received a payment of $3M. Blonn's complaint was not as serious as Walters,' so she asked only for $2M.

Two months later another Jameson employee came forward with a similar complaint against Harrington, this one more serious, and she asked for $4M. She also cited the Walters settlement.

Both of these new complaints went to Rapco's attorneys. They were frustrated that the Walters settlement had been leaked. They first thought Walters had given out the information, but further study showed that one of the secretaries in Rapco's attorneys' office had mentioned it to another Rapco employee, who in turn told several of her Rapco friends. Within three months of the settlement with Walters, the settlement amount and conditions were out in the Rapco conglomerate. The secretary who leaked the information was fired.

Now Rapco's attorneys had to begin their discussions about next steps – major damage control. They thought they could win in court in both the new cases, but the same questions came before them. Should they settle or go to trial? It did not help that a precedent had been set with the Walters case. Nevertheless, Rapco decided to fight the new claims in court. Eventually each of the claims went to court. Eventually each case was settled out of court with a $1.5M to each claimant. Not having funds to pay out the settlements, Rapco mortgaged one of its buildings to get the money needed.

Two more cases came to light in the next two years. The cases were settled for $250,000 each.

1. In retrospect, Jameson paid out $6.5M because of Harrington's misdeeds. Sentiment among Rapco's lawyers was they should have let the Walters case go to trial What are the considerations a company should consider when determining whether to fight a claim or offer a settlement out-of-court?

2. Should Rapco have paid out the settlement to Walters?

3. How long would Rapco's reputation been damaged if the case had gone to trial, if at all?

4. Where was Rapco's insurance in this discussion? Did Rapco have insurance to cover its employee's alleged misdeeds?

5. Should Rapco have gone after Harrington and tried to retrieve some money from him?

Analysis

Rapco's dilemma is not that unusual. Fight or Pay? Rapco (and Jameson) should have completed a financial analysis to estimate the costs to the company in brand erosion and/or loss of sales. While these estimates are merely a "best guess," experienced attorneys can come to a reasonable figure. Once the estimated costs have been determined, then the firm can decide whether to fight Walters' claim in court. Adding these two costs together, Rapco can determine if it would be better off financially to fight or cave to the request for compensation.

What Rapco did not know at the time of Walters' claim was that several other claims would be forthcoming. Once precedent had been set resolving Walters' claim, it was difficult to argue that the new claims should be fought in court, so Rapco paid the claims after getting them reduced somewhat.

No mention is made in the case whether Rapco or Jameson had insurance to cover employee misconduct. Also, the case does not tell us whether Rapco and Jameson had employee-training programs concerning sexual harassment. Having such programs in place gives some cover to the company that it was doing what it needed to do. If the company had provided training and it could be shown that Harrington had gone through the training, then the firm would have been in a better position to claim it had no guilt in the matter.

Attorneys have access to databases in which they can learn what typical payouts are in cases of this type that have court ordered settlements. Of course, many settlements made before court proceedings have non-disclosure agreements in place. Nevertheless, the payout to Walters seems excessively high. One wonders if Rapco's lawyers consulted these databases. Those data could have been used in negotiations between Rapco's and Walters' lawyers.

Case 3.8 Evaluating the CEO

Ralph Edwards was the CEO of a $100M firm in Alabama. He had been in office for five years. There was a general business recession starting about the same time Edwards took over as CEO. Fortunately, the general economy was gradually improving by the sixth year.

The firm had held its own during the recession. It had not grown in sales or profits, but it also had not dropped, which was better than some of the firm's main competitors. Under Edwards' leadership the firm had put a tight control on its expenses, and was able to weather the storm. Prospects for the future looked good.

Edwards was an articulate leader. He liked public events where he would shine. Over his years in office he held several extravaganzas, which gave opportunity to show off the firm and his leadership.

Edwards' management style was to keep tight rein on his direct reports. He liked to get into some of the details of the firm's management down two layers in the management structure. Some accused him of being a micro-manager.

Others viewed Edwards as a decision-maker who worked on his own. He made some enemies the first year by declaring several changes without consulting anyone. He unilaterally altered the public appearance of the firm by changing several marketing artifacts, such as the company colors, the company logo, the company song, and the marketing phrases used in advertising. The company banner was changed to make the firm appear less stodgy. Everyone admitted that each of these changes was fairly trivial, but believed the changes illustrated a non-consultative management style.

Edwards hired a firm to do a strategic plan for the physical facilities. The plan cost the firm several hundred thousand dollars at a time when budgets were tight. This resulted in considerable criticism from the management staff. He also developed a long-range plan for the future of the firm. He constructed a BHAG that called for the firm to quadruple in size in the next ten-year period. While many admitted the ideas generated were good, they didn't like the way Edwards went about putting the ideas in place.

The Board of Directors was around, but it was a large, pass-through, friendly board. The board came to town and spent time working on the agenda prepared by Edwards and the board chairperson. In effect, the Board meetings were directed by Edwards. The Board chair was a friendly man who did not like confrontation and wanted to keep harmony. There was an executive committee of the board that served as the personnel committee on behalf of the Board, but the basic board culture was pass-through, don't make waves.

Each year the firm did a satisfaction survey of its clients. Year after year the clients reported a good view of the firm, its CEO, and its senior leadership. Edwards sent a copy of the report to board members, who in turn gained a good view of Edwards' leadership.

In Edwards' fourth year it came time to renew his contract, which was to be a three-year extension. The board chair sent out a questionnaire to the firm's employees asking them to evaluate Edwards. The results of the survey were benign, so the board chairperson took a report to his executive committee, and then recommended to the entire board that Edwards be given a new three-year contract. That was done and the firm was ready to move into the future.

In the meantime, several thought leaders in the firm didn't think things were going all that well. They didn't understand the board's actions in continuing with Edwards, since they themselves had turned in negative responses to the board's questionnaire. These thought leaders started to talk more broadly to the firm's employees, got them stirred up, and many thought Edwards had to go.

The employees were stirred up, and decided to do something about it. They called a meeting of professional employees (contravening the employee handbook policies), expelled all senior administrators from the meeting, and had a long discussion about the CEO. The net result was a vote in which 70% voted no confidence in the CEO. The vote was transmitted to the board chair.

After much heartburn and several months of discussion, the board chair and the CEO determined it would be best for the CEO to go. An exit package was arranged, and the CEO was gone at the end of the fiscal year.

As you might imagine, there was much trauma in the firm because of these events. Sides were taken among the employees; many feelings were hurt. In later discussions between employees and board members, many board personnel claimed to have been out of the loop. They did not know what was happening at the firm nor about the unrest among the employees, and several put the onus on the chair and executive committee for letting things get out of hand. One person estimated the cost of the problem to have been about $1M.

Discussion Questions

1. How should the entire Board of Directors have been involved in evaluating the CEO?

2. How can a Board change its culture from being a pass-through board to a more engaged and action-oriented board?

3. What should the Board chair have done to conduct a better survey of Edwards' performance?

4. What should be the Board's stance with respect to run-of-the mill employees and their views of management?

5. Should Edwards have demanded a more comprehensive assessment of his performance?

Analysis

There were several failures along the line with respect to

Edwards' work and the assessment thereof. First to be mentioned is the Board, its culture, and its work on this particular assignment. It is noted that the Board was a pass-through board. Many of the members had little input or insight into the work of the firm. The Executive Committee had more direct input, and the Chair of the Board was the key person working with the firm's management. It is obvious that the Board should shake up its culture.

The Board should have had better insight into Edwards' work. The CEO should be monitored continuously, not just when it is time to renew the CEO's contract. The CEO should put in place mechanisms to take the temperature of all in the firm as to how the firm was doing and how its managers were performing.

In the case of the renewal process, the survey work to get information did not adequately consider the professional and rank-and-file employees. Subsequent events showed that those employees were deeply concerned about the CEO and his performance; a more adequate survey should have revealed the depth of those feelings.

The Board members could not keep silent about the situation. Many talked with rank-and-file employees after the blow-up and several remarked that they didn't know what was going on. Also, they effectively had little to say about the renewal contract that went sour. Board members should have training as to correct protocol for board member pronouncements.

Edwards himself was not without fault. Once he knew there was dissatisfaction in the ranks he should have been talking with the Board Chair about the matter and seeking corrective action.

The professional employees who called for a vote of no confidence were in the wrong. Because their meeting and action was against company policy, the Board could have ignored their concerns and vote. Also, it did not portend for good relationships downstream between management and workers.

Case 3.9: Hiring Decisions are Tough

Tim Davidson was an administrator of a small healthcare firm located in a small town with a population of 5,000. Davidson was dealing with attendance and performance issues with the facility's receptionist for some time. Davidson finally realized that she had a drinking problem, and eventually she resigned her position.

Davidson was anxious to get the position filled, as the receptionist's work was important to the firm. The receptionist's desk was located at the very front of the facility; the receptionist greeted visitors and handled the switchboard. Davidson posted the position on the facility's website as well as with the local Job Service agency.

That night, Davidson went home, and like any other night, shared some details about his day with his wife, Sharla, over dinner. Davidson shared the news about the receptionist, and told Sharla he has posted the position and was hoping to fill it quickly. Sharla commented that one of their friends, Lucy Jones, was looking for a job. Davidson was hesitant, as he knew Jones and was aware of some of her wild weekend behavior. Moreover, Davidson maintained a strict personal policy of not hiring family or friends.

Over the next week, Sharla kept hounding Davidson to hire Jones. Jones applied for the position, along with a couple of other potential candidates. Davidson was still hesitant. After he reviewed the applications, he decided that he should at least give

Jones a "courtesy interview" while interviewing two other applicants. Davidson created a small interview panel that included the bookkeeper, the office manager, and himself. After the interviews were complete, to Davidson's surprise, the bookkeeper and office manager liked Jones the best of the three candidates. He felt backed into a corner at this point, with pressure from his wife Sharla and now from the bookkeeper and office manager to hire Jones. He agreed, and offered Jones the job.

Things went well for a while. Jones passed the 90-day probationary period with flying colors, and she was then made a permanent employee. However, shortly thereafter, Jones' performance began to diminish. Her attendance began to suffer, especially on Mondays. She would often call in sick on Mondays or come in an hour or two late. As Davidson began addressing these performance issues with Jones, she was offended. She could not believe that Davidson would be so strict with her. After all, they were long-time family friends. Jones shared her frustrations with Davidson's wife Sharla. Now Davidson was getting it from both ends - attitude from Jones at work and attitude from Sharla at home. Davidsons felt trapped, and wondered why he went against his better judgement - and his personal rule of not hiring any family or friends.

Discussion Questions

1. Should Davidson have hired Jones? Why or why not?

2. What are the pros and cons of hiring a friend or personal acquaintance?

3. Could Davidson have assigned Jones to report to another person and thus avoided supervising a close friend?

4. Should Davidson have let his wife influence his hiring decision? Why or why not?

5. Could Davidson have set up a good job description with performance standards that would have given better guidance to Davidson and Jones regarding performance expectations?

Analysis

Davidson got himself into a real pickle when he hired his wife's close friend. He felt pressured to get someone into the position, and jumped at the one person who had applied and apparently met the position expectations.

There was no indication of a job description and statement of behavioral expectations. Having such in place might have headed off the problems that emerged.

Having to manage a close friend of the family was not a good position for Davidson. The friend thought Davidson should cut her some slack, and not hold her to strict employee standards. Taking advantage of the situation, Jones used her connection to Davidson's wife to put more pressure on Davidson to let up on his normal expectations for his employee.

Davidson could have gone to a temp agency to get

someone to fill in the position while he conducted a more thorough search for a permanent employee. He could have also made stronger cases for the other candidates that were interviewed for the receptionist position. He should not have hired a close friend of the family; if he did, he should have that person report to another manager.

Case 3.10: Hiring the New CEO

The Watsun Company was a 100-year-old, $45M firm on the west coast. It had a good reputation and was serving its customers well. For the past five years it had been growing around 3% per year in both revenues and profits.

The CEO had been in place for 10 years. He worked with a big board of directors. The board was largely a pass-through board, but there was a more active executive committee of the board. The CEO worked very closely with the board chairperson, Winston Graves. The CEO and Graves talked two or three times a week. The CEO didn't make a significant move without Graves giving advance approval. Graves was ensconced in place and had no reason to move on when the CEO retired.

The CEO announced his retirement nine months in advance of the effective retirement date. Graves appointed a small group of board members to be the eyes and ears of the board and to bring a CEO recommendation to the full board. Graves then hired an outside headhunter firm to search for the new CEO. The search was to be done in secret and was to last six months. The headhunters identified four potential CEOs who were interviewed by the board search committee in various airports around the country.

Toward the end of the six-month period a new candidate, Roger Bensen, was brought to the attention of the board committee, a candidate not proposed by the headhunter firm. Bensen was then the CEO of a similarly sized firm in the Midwest. He had been in place there for nine years and had done an excellent job as CEO. The firm Bensen headed had grown 40% in the years he was in charge.

Bensen was a charismatic leader. He was tall, handsome, an excellent public speaker, dressed very well, had a beautiful wife and four good-looking children, all in high school or college. Bensen met people well and those people who talked with Bensen came away feeling that Bensen was a best friend.

The board committee decided to interview Bensen, which they did at the St. Louis airport. Committee members were blown away by Bensen; they just knew Bensen was the man for the next era at Watsun. The board search committee contacted Graves, who in turn conducted a mail ballot and the board unanimously elected Bensen to be the new CEO.

In a few months Bensen moved to town and took up his new duties. He took the town by storm, and everything started off well. Then, about five months into Bensen's leadership, Bensen decided to move the firm from its then-current location to a new location about 10 miles away. Bensen took his C-level leadership team to the new site and told them about the move. Unfortunately, he didn't tell Graves, who found out about it through the grapevine. Graves was not at all happy.

In fact, Graves and Benson were not on the same page at all. Benson's philosophy of working with the board was to keep the board away from the firm, keep it out of town, and have only the minimum number of board meetings each year required by law. Benson didn't talk to the board chair very often, and he felt that the board should let Benson do his job and keep out of his hair. As one might imagine, this approach was not to Grave's liking, since he had been very active in his work with the previous CEO.

When Graves found out about the proposed move, he became unglued. He and Benson had a knock-down argument about the management of the firm. This led to further confrontations and distance between Graves and Bensen. In another couple of months Graves had had it with Benson and decided Benson had to go. Graves worked out an exit agreement with Benson, and Benson was gone before his first anniversary with the company.

Discussion Questions

1. Why did the Board skip over the recommendations of the headhunter firm?

2. What advice would you give to a hiring group that would keep them from considering attributes that were mainly surface-level features?

3. What were the reasons the Board rushed into a decision about a new CEO?

4. How could the Board have learned more about Benson's management philosophy, and especially his philosophy of working with the

Board?

5. How could Benson have learned more about Watsun's management culture?

Analysis

What went wrong, and was there any blame for the short-term tenure of the CEO? Yes, both the board and Benson were in the wrong in that they didn't do their homework before Benson was hired. It turns out that Benson was managing at Watsun the same way he managed at his previous firm. Benson didn't change his philosophy nor his approach. The board committee didn't go deep enough into Benson's history and qualifications to determine how he managed. They were getting close to the end of the period they had set for finding a new CEO; they found a charismatic leader and jumped at the chance of bringing Benson on board. They just didn't do their homework.

Similarly, Benson didn't go deep enough into the management culture at Watsun, and found himself in an environment and working with people who were on a different page in their understandings and experience of how Watsun should be managed. He and Chairperson Graves didn't go through a courtship phase to find out about each other, their expectations and approaches to management of the firm. Benson didn't do his homework.

In summary, Watsun lost a year of leadership. The board had to do another search, pay out more money for the second search, and forewent opportunities for moving the firm ahead.

Case 3.11: Keep Your Customers or Not?

Merk Foods was a small, thriving food distributorship located in the Sandeen Valley in Utah. Merk sold food products to large retail chain stores in the state as well as to small to medium sized restaurants, delis, and eateries. The company did about $5 million in sales annually, and had a staff of 12 including the CEO, an office manager (who also served as the bookkeeper), a warehouse manager, and nine sales and delivery associates. The company was doing well financially, and the office manager stayed on top of accounts receivable to ensure timely payment for goods was received.

Prior to the office manager coming on board, the company did not have a full-time bookkeeper. Paperwork was a mess, accounts had not been looked at for some time, and collections had not been organized for years. The new office manager worked through these issues and had everything well straightened out within a year.

One customer, York Deli, had racked up quite an outstanding balance on its account due to several checks bouncing over a period of several months. This was prior to the new office manager being hired. The account had a past due balance in excess of $21,000. The CEO had told the owner of York Deli that he would no longer accept checks from them, and instead they would have to pay cash on delivery. This arrangement worked well for a period of time. However, one day the owner of the Deli placed a big order, and when the Merk delivery associate delivered the product, the owner of the deli stated that he didn't have cash because he forgot to go to the bank. He offered to write a check. Knowing that this was a "cash only" customer, the delivery associate called the CEO of Merk to see if it would be okay to accept a check this time. The CEO agreed, and the delivery associate delivered the $2,000 order in exchange for the check.

Within a few days the office manager received a notice from the bank stating that the check from York Deli was returned for insufficient funds. The office manager immediately notified the CEO of the situation, and the CEO received the news with disbelief. He was certain after all the previous issues that this would not happen again. The office manager suggested suspending all future product deliveries until the account was brought current, as now York Deli owed Merk nearly $54,000. The CEO ignored the office manager's recommendation and instructed her to continue deliveries to York Deli but to maintain the "cash only" policy without exception.

The office manager could not understand the CEO's rationale for continuing to deliver products to a customer with a delinquent account balance of over $54,000. During a lunch between the two the next day, the office manager asked the CEO why he still delivered product to York Deli in spite of their exceedingly high delinquent balance. His argument was that he felt like he had a better chance of recouping payment for the past due invoices if he maintained a business relationship with the deli.

A couple of months later, while York Deli had been

making cash payments for their new product deliveries as agreed upon, there was no additional payments made toward the outstanding balance. Soon after, York Deli stopped ordering product from Merk, and Merk never recovered any of the outstanding delinquent balance from York Deli.

Discussion Questions

1. How far behind should a company let a customer get before stopping selling to the customer?

2. After it stopped taking checks from York Deli, Merk still delivered for cash. Was that a good decision?

3. How should Merk have gone after York Deli's delinquent account?

4. After York Deli quit buying from Merk, should Merk have instituted legal proceedings against York Deli?

5. Why did the CEO want to continue with York Deli? Was York Deli such a big customer that losing the deli would be a hard blow to Merk?

Analysis

It appears that Merk did not have a firm policy concerning delinquent accounts; Merk was making up policy on the fly and then not sticking to the policy. There was a conflict of opinion between the CEO and the office manager over the practice.

The story does not tell us the time period over which York Deli's account went delinquent. A good policy would include a section on timeliness of payments due to Merk.

What did Merk do with the check returned for insufficient funds? Did Merk run it through again? Did Merk have a pow-wow with York Deli to try to resolve the check issue? Did Merk have to pay the bank for processing the bad check?

At the end of the day, businesses need to maintain profitability. If customers are out of compliance with payment policies, or are delinquent in paying their bills, consequences need to be exercised per company policy.

Case 3.12: A New Gang in Town

Wilderness Cycles, Inc. was a $25M firm that sold specialty bicycles. Bicycles sold from $700 to $8000, with the average sale being $1350. Wilderness had 30 employees in its retail outlet in downtown Seattle. As this story begins, Wilderness was 60 years old, having started just after WWII. Many third-generation customers loyally supported Wilderness because of its excellent customer service. Wilderness started out as a family run partnership, but soon converted into a corporation. After being run by family members for 27 years, Wilderness hired an outsider to become CEO who managed the company for 33 years. At the firm's 60-year mark he retired and a new CEO was brought in.

The new CEO saw opportunities for added scope to the company. Further, he had a nagging worry that the bicycle business might not be sustainable over the next 20 years. He decided to expand the business by starting to sell ATVs. In his mind the product fit well with specialty bicycles, the customer fit was good, and new business would be brought to the firm.

To this end, he divided the business into two divisions, the bicycle division and the ATV division. He appointed division managers for the two sectors. On the ATV side, he signed contracts with three ATV manufacturers and started to sell and service their ATVs. Twenty employees, several of them ATV mechanics, were hired. Wilderness spent considerable money advertising its new products.

Problems started to emerge soon after the new division was created. Personnel from the bicycle division began to resent the attention the ATV people were getting. The bicycle people viewed themselves as the true Wilderness people; from their perspective, the bicycle division was the real heart and soul of the company. The new people were interlopers. Further, the ATV mechanics did not dress like the bicycle people did, a detail that the bicycle people often talked about. The bicycle folks seemed to nag about every little change the ATV folks made.

The ATV people reciprocated with bad feelings toward the old-timer bicycle nerds. The ATV division needed more space, which the bicycle folks didn't want to give up. The ATV people wanted to adjust business hours, which the bicycle folks didn't want to do. The ATV side wanted new financing arrangements for its customers, and that upset the bicyclists. To top it all off, the two division managers didn't get along.

Five years after bringing in the ATV division, the firm was doing quite well overall. Annual revenues were pushing $45M, $24M from the ATV division and $21M from the bicycle division. The bicycle folks were distraught at the dip in bicycle revenues, while the ATV folks crowed about how good their side of the house was doing. The internal culture wars were going full blast, while there was frost between the two divisions.

Discussion Questions

1. How could the CEO have better prepared the

bicycle people to receive the new ATV Division?

2. How could the CEO have mitigated the bad feelings between the two division heads?

3. What could have been done with the ATV Division people to get them to quit deprecating the Bicycle Division side of the company?

4. What could the CEO do to make the bicycle people feel more wanted and appreciated?

5. Overall, what strategies could the CEO have implemented to more effectively lead people through this big change in the company?

Analysis

The CEO should have worked extensively with the bicycle people to educate them why the new division was needed. He should have foreseen the difficulties that might emerge and tried to head them off before they turned into reality. It's sort of like a new baby coming into the family; the existing children need to be educated and prepared for the new addition.

Now that the problem has emerged, the CEO should work with the two division heads to reconcile their differences and get them to work together more effectively. The two division heads will be very important in bringing the two divisions back into a working team. The CEO may have to knock heads to get the two division chiefs singing on the same page. If necessary, one or both of the division heads may need to be replaced.

The CEO and the Bicycle Division head need to work together to make the bicycle people feel more appreciated. They should get recognition for the work they are doing. Any perks that have been given to the ATV side should also be given to the bicycle side. Programs that make the ATV side more lucrative should be considered for the bicycle side as well.

The CEO and division heads should introduce social events that bring the personnel from the two divisions together. Company picnics, contests, family recognitions, and lots of information flow should be instituted.

It will probably take a few years of hard work to bring the people of the two divisions to feel good about each other. Failure to put a good culture in place will result in more problems downstream.

Case 3.13: The No Guts Leader

Weston Electronics was a small manufacturer of electronic measuring devices. It had a 50-year history, starting out as an electricity service company working for customers in the Albany area. Over time it migrated to manufacturing and now made switches and meters.

Weston produced two main types of product. The customers for the two groups of products had very little overlap, and the factory had two main production lines for the two groups. In one of his periodic restructures of the firm, the CEO decided to divide the company into two main groups. He convinced the friendly board to make the change, then named two insiders to Vice Presidencies, each responsible for one of the groups.

The two new VPs were good guys, let's call them Jim and Frank. Both were well liked by employees and their peers. Both had been around for 15 or more years and knew the business backward and forward. They got along well together.

After that the similarity ended. Jim was a thinker. He liked to mull things over and take his time about making decisions. He wanted all the facts, and didn't like surprises. In a typical meeting with one of his direct reports, he would answer a question arising from the report that he would think it over and get back to the questioner in a few days. It would take several weeks of meetings before Jim would give an answer.

Frank was just the opposite. He was decisive. He didn't need all the facts to make a decision. When he had the important facts and could see a way forward, he would make a decision. In a typical meeting with one of his direct reports, almost all the report's requests would be answered on the spot. At most it would take a week for Frank to have an answer ready.

After six months into the new administrative structure, the rumor mill among the employees was that Frank was a good person to lead, while Jim was taking way too long to make decisions. People who technically reported to Jim started to go to Frank to get directions. Frank became the *de facto* leader of the firm.

Jim was getting more and more uncomfortable in his new role. He couldn't stand the pressure of all these decisions that were being thrown his way. Things got so bad that eight months into the new job Jim had a nervous breakdown and had to take a leave from work for three months. When he returned he resigned from the leadership position, and fortunately for him, there was an opening back in the office he had left to become VP. He became a happy man again.

The CEO repented of his decision to split the firm into two parts, and went back to a single operations head for the firm. Frank got the job.

Discussion Questions

1. How did the CEO vet Jim and Frank for their jobs? One appeared to be well suited, while the other was not.

2. What was the CEO's decision-making style? Did

he mull things over for a long time before coming to a decision, or was he decisive and/or quick?

3. When do you think Jim realized that he was not cut out for the new leadership position?

4. Would the CEO have cut Jim loose from the firm if there had not been a spot to which Jim could return?

5. How could Jim have determined in advance that the leadership position was not his cup of tea?

Analysis

The CEO made a serious mistake when he appointed Jim to the leadership spot. Jim was not psychologically equipped for the job, and the CEO could have determined that in advance.

Jim made a mistake by accepting the leadership position. He should have known, or could have found out in advance, that the promotion was not going to work out.

There are various assessments and evaluations available that could have been used with the two potential appointees. The CEO should have required those evaluations, and the two potential appointees should have requested such.

Jim was fortunate that there was a spot available for him to return to his old job. Jim was also fortunate that he had not burned his bridges while spending several months in the leadership position; the CEO and others were ready to welcome him back. Jim dodged a bullet.

Case 3.14: Opportunity Comes Knocking

Sam Carlson was the finance manager of a small professional services firm that provided services to people with disabilities. The firm had an administrator, a finance manager, and a few other management positions. The firm reported to a larger parent company that was headquartered out of state, but the facility was largely autonomous. However, financial reporting rolled up to the parent company and annual audits were completed through the parent company. There was also a national-level accounting firm that audited the books each year.

After Carlson had been working for the firm for a while, he learned the systems and processes and realized how little oversight there was of his role. The administrator briefly scanned and signed off on the monthly financial statements, and they were then sent to headquarters. The annual audit consisted of a questionnaire that Carlson had to fill out along with some copies of test transactions that were selected by the auditors for review.

Carlson was living beyond his means, and aspired to make home improvements to his aging house. His wife didn't work outside the home, so Carlson was the sole breadwinner of the household. He began to make purchases of a personal nature on company accounts. It didn't look suspicious, as Carlson often went to town to purchase various supplies for the firm. He would purchase items for his home from established vendors that the firm has done business with for some time. He would simply give the receipts to the accounts payable clerk and ask her to pay them. Even the administrator didn't notice anything unusual during his cursory monthly reviews of the financial statements. Nothing looked out of order.

One day, Carlson became too comfortable in his scheming, and decided to up the ante. He had heard many stories of people setting up bogus vendors and being caught, so he shied away from that approach. Instead, he decided he would open up a credit card in the firm's name. With his status as financial manager, he was able to do so.

Once he received the credit card, he began making purchases of a personal nature. Again, he would use vendors that were familiar to the company, so no one was the wiser. He would purchase hardware and tools from the local hardware store, he would pay for extravagant weekend hotel stays and rental cars, and claim them as business-related. Over a period of several years, Carlson racked up expenses to the tune of $30,000 - mostly small purchases that flew under the radar. However, it just so happened that Carlson got to be lackadaisical in his approach, and made a purchase at a spa using the credit card. Again, the bookkeeper did not think anything of it. She supposed it was an employee gift or something, and the administrator only saw the vendor's name on the monthly financial statements, and that did not seem out of the ordinary. However, during a subsequent annual audit, one of the few transactions that the auditors randomly selected as a test was this particular month's credit card bill. Carlson pulled all of the documentation that the auditors requested, and reviewed it. He noticed the receipt from the spa that showed all of the specifics of the transaction - customer name (Carlson), the date, the services provided, and the cost. Carlson quickly became nervous, as he knew that this might be the end of his little charade...and his job. He destroyed the back-up documentation and indicated on the credit card statement that the receipt had "been lost."

Weeks later as the auditors reviewed the information, they came across the credit card statement that was lacking documentation. The auditor thought that it was strange, as usually all of the financial transactions from this facility had detailed documentation. The auditor decided to call Carlson to discuss the transaction. Carlson happened to be out to lunch, and the bookkeeper answered the phone. The auditor explained the situation to the bookkeeper, and asked if she could help clarify the expense. Not only could the bookkeeper clarify the expense, but she was able to provide a copy of the original receipt. Apparently, the bookkeeper scanned all copies of receipts to her computer when she would receive them from the firm's staff. The bookkeeper emailed the receipt from the spa purchase, with all of its detail to the auditor. This led to a full-scale audit of Carlson's credit card charges for the year. It did not take long for the Administrator to call Carlson in and serve him termination papers. The company did not chase Carlson to get the money back because it didn't want to get bad publicity and alarm the investors.

Discussion Questions

1. Why did the administrator not pay more

attention to Carlson's finance reports?

2. What could the firm have done to assure that Carlson's expenditures were business expenses and not personal expenses?

3. Where did the parent company go wrong in setting up a culture and system that would allow a Carlson to spend the company's money on his personal interests?

4. How could the internal audits have been set up to catch malfeasances such as Carlson's?

5. How should the bookkeeper have been trained to look for problem spending?

Analysis

Carlson ran off the rails. He clearly committed a felony by misusing the company's money. His personal ethics were lacking; he should have known better and not let himself get in the financial situation he was in.

The company was at fault in several ways. The administrator of the local firm was lackadaisical in his approach to the company's records. The bookkeeper had not been trained to examine the reimbursement requests when they came by her desk, and her job description did not have a provision for blowing the whistle on such problems.

The parent company's audit system did not catch the problem for several years. Further, the outside national accounting firm did not catch the problem. There must be internal controls in place to reduce and eliminate opportunities for fraud such as this. That said, internal controls are usually challenging to implement in a small firm.

Altogether, the company culture was such that a system of trust had been established in which supervisors did not closely examine the financial dealings of their direct reports. While trust is a good thing when it comes to working relationships, it cannot absolve people from accountability. Accountability systems must be put into place, even in the most trusting business environments.

The company should have chased Carlson for a return of the money. The chasing process did not have to be public unless Carlson made it so. If the investors found out about the problem, they would probably have been happy to know the firm was a good steward of its resources.

Case 3.15: Keep Up with Your Customers

Whitcom & Sons, Inc. was a small manufacturing firm based in Akron, Ohio. Whitcom's annual revenues were close to $51M. There were 300 employees, 200 in manufacturing and 100 in administration and sales. The firm was 63 years old and enjoyed a good reputation in the Akron area. Its main output was bicycle frames. Ninety percent of its customers were east of the Mississippi, mostly in the Midwest and South. Ninety percent of its sales went to bicycle shops and bicycle assemblers.

Five years ago, Whitcom conceived and developed a new bicycle frame, called the Z-frame, that got very good reviews and became very popular. At that time Whitcom's revenues jumped from $40M to $46M in a two-year period. Whitcom built a new assembly plant at that time which well supported the then current level of sales.

Whitcom's CEO, David Rustlo, thought this would be a good time to expand Whitcom's assembly operations even further. Rustlo wanted expanded facilities to produce more Z-frames. He believed he could keep his current customers and add many new customers. Further, he believed those new customers would be similar to his current customers. He sold to Whitcom's Board of Directors the idea of building a new $8M facility that would be geared mainly to bicycle frames. Machinery, fixtures, and equipment for the building would cost another $4M.

Whitcom's sales had been level for two years, but

Whitcom argued that with expanded facilities for production and an expanded sales force the firm could substantially drive up sales of bicycle frames. With the Board's approval Rustlo went ahead with the expansion, focusing the building and equipment on the bicycle frame business. Additional production workers and salespersons were hired and turned loose to bring in the revenues.

Whitcom's employees liked the new facilities; company morale got a real boost. Visitors and prospective clients were impressed by the company, its facilities, and its campus. Ongoing clients liked what they saw. Unfortunately, for Whitcom and Rustlo, sales did not grow as envisioned. Whitcom was able to hang on to most of its traditional customers, but not many new customers were onboarded.

So Rustlo regretted his decision to expand his facilities. He was now stuck with a very nice building. The machinery equipment was so specialized that little of it could be used in other types of metal production work. Rustlo was faced with a flat revenue stream, about $51M a year, but he had a significant debt to pay for the new digs. To respond, Rustlo laid off most of the expanded workforce, and company morale sunk.

Discussion Questions

1. How could Rustlo have been more on top of predictions about the popularity of bicycles in particular and recreational equipment in general?

2. Do you think Rustlo did a market study to learn what the market wanted in terms of recreational equipment?

3. What makes a company build for the future based on its past success?

4. Could Whitcom have built a new facility but not have it so specialized it was good for only one thing?

5. What risk management strategies could have been employed to minimize the risk of this expansion endeavor?

Analysis

Rustlo did not do an adequate market analysis of the bicycle frame business. Level sales for the previous two years before the expansion should have been a strong signal that the bicycle frame business was maxing out. A good market study would have told him that customer demand for bicycles had peaked nationally, and especially in the Midwest and South. People were using discretionary money to purchase other types of recreational equipment.

Managers who rely too heavily on past data may be surprised by the future. The past certainly should be studied, but major ventures should be preceded by good market studies and risk analysis. Your customers from the past may stick with your firm because of past loyalty, but you may not gain new customers in a shifting market. Rustlo belatedly learned that it normally takes more than new facilities to bring in a substantial number of new customers.

Another mistake Rustlo made was to build new facilities that were focused on one particular product. Rather than buying machinery that could be used to fabricate many different types of steel products, Rustlo particularized on machinery that built bicycle frames very well. When the bicycle frame business soured, Rustlo was left holding the bag with unusable machinery.

Case 3.16: Risk Mismanagement

Jerry Curtis was the owner of A-1 Carpet, a full-service carpet retailer that specializes in whole-home carpet replacement. Curtis had 12 employees who usually worked in pairs, and six large trucks to deliver new carpet to customers and take away old carpet for disposal. All six of the trucks were large, but were just under the weight limit to be considered "commercial." Therefore, drivers were not required to hold a Commercial Driver's License (CDL).

One of Curtis' longtime friends, Shane Blanchard, had just sold his house and purchased a new one. He was all set to move over a weekend, but really did not want to make several trips with his small pickup truck, and he did not want to spend the money to rent a U-Haul truck. Blanchard wondered if Curtis might let him borrow one of his company trucks over the weekend for the move. He thought that would be perfect because A-1 Carpet is closed over the weekend and so it would not need the truck.

Blanchard phoned Curtis and asked him to meet for coffee. During their discussion, Blanchard shared all about his challenges with the move this far, and then he popped the question. Blanchard asked if he could borrow one of Curtis' company trucks to move with over the weekend. Curtis was initially hesitant, as he was unsure of the insurance issues that might exist. However, Blanchard finally convinced him, and Curtis agreed to let Blanchard borrow the truck for the weekend.

They arranged for Blanchard to stop by the office at 6pm on Friday to get the keys from Curtis. As Blanchard was leaving, Curtis jokingly said, "Please be careful, and don't crash my truck!" Blanchard assured him that the truck was in good hands.

Blanchard was excited to get home so he could start loading up the truck. He had a few friends coming over to help him pack up the furniture and load the truck, and Blanchard remembered that he had agreed to pay them each $50 for the help. Blanchard checked his wallet, but he only had $20, so he decided to stop by the bank to get more cash.

By this time, it was 6:20 pm, and the bank was closed. Therefore, Blanchard decided to go through the ATM lane at the bank. He did not even think about the size of the truck he was driving when he pulled around to the back of the bank. As he pulled up to the bank's ATM machine, he heard a loud crash and the truck abruptly stopped in its tracks. Blanchard had hit the overhead roof of the bank that covers the ATM machines. This resulted in tens of thousands of dollars in damage to the truck and the bank. While A-1 Carpet had a good auto insurance policy on its truck fleet, the policy explicitly listed the drives that were covered – only the employees of the company. Therefore, the damages that occurred during the time Blanchard borrowed the truck were not covered by insurance. Had Blanchard been an employee of A-1 Carpet, the insurance policy would have covered the damage.

Discussion Questions

1. Did A-1 Carpet have a policy in place that dealt with loaning out company trucks? If so, did Curtis violate the policy?

2. Did Blanchard have insurance that covered other-owned vehicles he might be driving?

3. Are there any conditions in which Curtis might have let Blanchard use the truck so that Blanchard's driving was covered by insurance?

4. How was Curtis going to get money from Blanchard? Was that going to wreck their friendship?

5. How could Curtis have better managed risk while at the same time maintaining good relationship with Blanchard?

Analysis

Blanchard should not have asked Curtis to loan him a truck. That was pushing the friendship too far. While Blanchard probably thought little of the potential risk to A-1 Carpet, he should have realized he was putting Curtis in a precarious position.

Curtis should not have loaned the truck to Blanchard without assuring that the truck was fully covered when driven by Blanchard.

A-1 Carpet should have in place policies regarding the use of company trucks. Such a policy could be used by Curtis to turn down requests to borrow company trucks by Blanchard or others.

Companies must consider all of the risks involved in decisions such as this. Risk management is a key role of any manager in a company –especially an owner of a small company that lacks the capital and resources to be able to compensate for occasional deviances in risk management.

Case 3.17: Safety Rules vs. Recommendations

Jason Marks was a great employee at Lumber Leader, a local, small-chain hardware and lumber store. Marks was a high school student who worked about 30 hours per week. Marks was frequently scheduled for the closing shift, since he attended school during the day. Wendy Weaver, one of the assistant managers who frequently worked the closing shift, was particularly fond of Marks and liked his willingness to help wherever and whenever. The store had established strict safety rules and guidelines, one of which included a rule that no one under the age of 18 could work in the lumber department. The lumber department provided several hazardous services such as cutting lumber for customers using high-powered saws as well as cutting and threading galvanized pipe and other metal using high-powered machinery.

Among the responsibilities of closing the lumber department was cleaning the equipment and bringing in all outdoor merchandise displays at the end of the night. This included the task of bringing in pallets of promotional material that the store placed outside by the front doors each morning. Pallets would include 2-cubic-foot bags of mulch, 60-pound bags of concrete, 5-gallon trees and shrubs, and a variety of other merchandise. This required that the employee closing the lumber department would need to drive the forklift out of the lumber department's large roll-up door, down the alley about 100 feet, and to the front door area to pick up each pallet. The employee would then drive the pallet into the lumber department and place it in one of the aisles, where the morning crew would then take the pallet back outside first thing prior to the store opening.

On occasion, the employee scheduled to close the lumber department called in sick. Marks willingly volunteered to work the lumber department that evening, even though he was only 17 years old. After a few attempts to call in employees to cover the shift, Weaver decided to let Marks work the department that night. Marks had shadowed lumber employees in the past, so was familiar with how to work the equipment. However, Weaver was adamant that Marks not use any equipment and call her if a customer needed any cutting services or if the forklift was needed. This happened on several occasions over the period of a few months, and Weaver grew more comfortable with Marks in the lumber department. Eventually, Weaver allowed Marks to start cutting materials for customers as well as operating the forklift to bring in the outside merchandise pallets at the end of the night.

One night, Marks was assisting a customer right up to closing time with some intricate cuts of wood. After he was done, he walked the customer up to customer service, where the cashiers were already counting their tills as it was a few minutes after closing time. Marks ran back to the lumber department and started the forklift in order to bring the outside merchandise in from the front of the store. Normally there were not many customers in the store during the last 30 minutes of business hours, so Marks was able to get most of the outdoor merchandise into the lumber department by the time the store closed. Since it was already late, he was in a hurry to bring in the merchandise. He opened the large roll-up door to the lumber department. However, in the rush of the moment, he did not open the door all the way. Marks then proceeded to drive the forklift out the door, and the upper frame of the forklift crashed into the door, causing the door to come off the tracks and come crashing down on the forklift. The crash could be heard throughout the store. Weaver came rushing back to see what had happened. Thankfully, Marks was not injured in the incident, but the lumber department roll up door was a total loss.

Now the store could not be secured for the evening due to the incident, so Weaver had to call a 24-hour security company to send a security guard to protect the store from intrusion overnight. While Marks was written up for poor safety procedures, Weaver was subsequently fired for breaking company policy and letting a 17-year-old employee work in the lumber department and operate the forklift.

Discussion Questions

1. Should the process of dealing with the pallets been modified?

2. How can a company set its policies and procedures to be assured unauthorized people do not use dangerous equipment?

3. What procedures should a company put in place to assure that trained employees are in place at all times the business is open?

4. Should the company have fired Weaver? Should

the company have fired Marks?

5. How can organizations ensure that mangers do not expose the company to undue risk such as this?

Analysis

The procedures used for closing up the shop should have been altered. It appears the employees wanted to get away the moment the store was closed for business, and get everything buttoned up before closing time. The outside displays should not be brought in until after the business is closed.

Weaver let Marks operate dangerous equipment without adequate training. The company should have a training protocol that employees would go through to be taught how to use the equipment safely. Only after the employee has gone through the training and been approved should the employee be allowed to use the dangerous equipment. This would apply to both the cutting tools and the forklifts. Weaver should not have allowed Marks to use the equipment. A further complication was the Marks was not 18, so Weaver violated the company policy in that regard.

Marks himself was not completely at fault. He had an attitude of helpfulness that all appreciated. However, he also should have known the policies about working the cutting equipment and should not have volunteered to use the equipment while under age.

Case 3.18: Scaring the Customers

Amy Tucker was a receptionist at Weinstock Consulting Group, Inc. One of the principals of the group told Tucker that he was going to buy lunch for the office, and asked Tucker to take orders and pick up the food. There were only five people in the office that day, so it was not going to be a particularly large order. Tucker proceeded to get everyone's order and walked across the street to Juicy Burger, a local fast-food establishment.

As Tucker walked up to the counter to place the order, Tim Hyslop, a new employee who had been working at Juicy Burger for about two weeks, greeted her. As Tucker placed the order, Hyslop was taking quite a long time to find the food items on his computer screen. In one instance, Tucker asked for no onions or pickles, and extra mustard on one of the burgers. This seemed to stump Hyslop, who kept on asking Tucker to repeat herself as he tried to find the right buttons on the computer screen. After some time, the order was complete, and Tucker waited patiently for the food.

As Hyslop called Tucker's number, she walked up to receive her order. While Tucker had placed the order "to go," it was prepared as if it was going to be eaten in the restaurant, presented on two trays. She told Hyslop that she wanted the food "to go." As Hyslop prepared to place the food in bags, Tucker noticed that some of the items were wrong. There was a chicken sandwich on the tray, which was curious because Tucker ordered all hamburgers. She began showing Hyslop the mistake. At this time, the restaurant manager, Antonio

Guido, walked up and wondered what the problem was. As Tucker explained some of the issues with the order, Guido became very angry.

Guido started yelling at Hyslop stating, "You always mess up the orders!" Hyslop apologized profusely to both Tucker and Guido. Guido continued his rant: "I don't know why I hired you in the first place. I knew it was going to be a mistake! Get back on the register and take orders!" At this point, all of the customers and employees in the restaurant had stopped what they were doing to observe the commotion. Guido was so upset that he was having a hard time opening the bags properly. He ripped one bag trying to open it, and subsequently crumbled it up with his hand and threw it at Hyslop. At this point Tucker felt terrible for getting Hyslop in so much trouble. She told Guido "It is really okay – it's not that big of a deal," to which Guido responded, "No, it's my fault. I shouldn't have hired an incompetent idiot."

Finally, Tucker's order was bagged up. She quickly left the restaurant feeling terrible about how Guido treated Hyslop. As she was on the brink of tears, she vowed to herself that she would never return to Juicy Burger.

Discussion Questions

1. If Guido thought that Hyslop was incompetent, why did Guido hire him in the first place?

2. Should Guido have trained Hyslop better before allowing him to take customers' orders by

himself?

3. How should Guido have addressed the issues with Hyslop?

4. What could Guido have done to turn Tucker from a disgruntled customer into a delighted customer?

5. Now that Guido had denigrated Hyslop, what should Guido do to correct the situation?

Analysis

Guido was out of control. He should not have hollered at Hyslop in front of customers; in fact, he should not yell at Hyslop even behind closed doors.

We need to go back to the beginning. How did Guido screen applicants for the job? Was there a better way to screen and hire applicants in order to select only the best candidates?

What kind of training program did Guido have for Hyslop? Was the training thorough enough and long enough that Guido could turn Hyslop loose to take customer orders on his own? If Hyslop messed up orders, did Guido have a retraining program available?

Since the order was messed up so much, Guido could have given the order to Tucker without charge. That might have changed Tucker from a frustrated buyer to a delighted customer. He could have given Tucker a coupon for a next order to try to lure her back to Juicy Burger.

Case 3.19: School Zone in the Red Zone

A local school district was growing fast due to the rapid population growth within the district's boundaries. The two existing high schools were busting at the seams with student. Each had resorted to placing a number of portable classroom trailers in the parking lots. Something had to be done.

The School Board decided that the construction of a third high school within the district was a priority. As such, they presented a bond initiative to the community; it secured the required two-thirds votes, and it passed. Among other things included in the multi-million-dollar bond initiative was approximately $40 million for the construction of the new high school.

The $40 million budget included all professional services needed for the project (architect, general contractor, etc.) as well as construction costs. The budget also included funds for furniture, fixtures, and supplies to get the school opened and ready to serve students. State law prohibited the use of bond funds for operational costs, so the budget only contained costs to get the school up and running. The school district appointed a principal over the high school who would lead the transition of faculty and staff coming from the two existing high schools in the district.

The 24-month project was nearing completion, and the district was preparing the budget for the upcoming school year. The new high school was scheduled to be completed in the summer, and would be ready to open upon the start of the new school year. During budget planning sessions, the principal identified several operational needs once the school would open. These operational needs included utilities, maintenance and custodial services, grounds maintenance, as well as other ancillary and support services such as equipment and technology. As the budget department crunched the numbers, it appeared that these costs would reach approximately $1.6 million for the first year.

Furthermore, it was realized that the third high school would actually generate no additional revenue to the school district. The funding that the state provided to school districts was based on the Average Daily Attendance (ADA) of students. Since students would be shifted from the two existing high schools to the new high school, this revenue had already been realized regardless of the opening of a new facility or not. The only hope the school district had was to gain additional new students to the district - that would lead to increased revenue generation.

The district gained approximately 100 new students that year, which resulted in additional revenue. However, it fell far short of the needed $1.6 million for Year-1 operating costs for the new year. The district found itself in financial distress over the lack of planning for operational costs for the new high school.

Discussion Questions

1. What could the Board of Trustees have done to count the costs and determine the potential income before the project began?

2. Could the Board of Trustees had done "what-if" analyses to determine the impacts of increased or decreased enrollments, and potential increases or decreases in state funding?

3. How could the principal have impacted the discussions in advance with identifying the critical operational needs for the new building?

4. What are some planning strategies that could have been employed to avoid this seemingly surprising revelation of operational costs?

5. Considering that students for the new high school were coming from the existing two high schools in the district, how could the district have redistributed funds to the new school to offset these initial start-up costs?

Analysis

This situation happens quite often. Building projects are begun without fully counting the cost or having the money in hand. Borrowing then has to occur against current income or from outside sources. Borrowing from ongoing budgets leaves those budgets strapped, and the budget squeeze may last for years.

It may be that the project was well planned out and the funds secured, provided business was normal and usual. Then something untoward happens, such as a downturn in enrollments, or a downturn in tax income, or changes in the formula for state reimbursement. The income sources that were to have supported the project deteriorate, and the project owners are left holding the bag.

Sometimes the project's owners cover the cost of the building, but don't take into consideration the secondary and tertiary impacts. Sometimes they forget to include money for equipping and furnishing the building. Sometimes they forget to consider long-term maintenance and upkeep of the building. Sometimes they forget to consider the costs of moving from the old facilities and the cost of tearing down or renovating the old facilities. Sometimes the costs of operating the new and improved building(s) are forgotten.

School Boards, superintendents, principals, and CFOs often get into trouble politically over a failed building project. This is often when trustees are voted out, or school administrators are reassigned or fired.

Case 3.20: Settling for a Mediocre C-Suite

Midway Homes was a mid-sized firm in Kentucky that built upscale homes. Midway typically built 100 homes a year, most in the price range of a half-million dollars and up. Most of the business was on the Kentucky side of the Ohio River, across from Cincinnati, and near Lexington.

Business had been decent. Midway muddled through the 2008 recession for four years, then business started to pick up in 2012. By 2015 profits were growing at about 6% a year. The founder of the closely held firm, Bobby Hendrix, decided to retire and move the firm outside the family, so he started looking for a new CEO.

Midway was organized into three divisions, each headed by a Vice President. The three VPs had been in place at least five years. All were reasonably competent and did their respective jobs reasonably well. They were all friends and socialized often with each other's families.

Hendrix considered each of these VPs to be the new CEO, but just didn't feel right about appointing one of them. He thought the VPs were competent, but they didn't have the energy and vision to be CEO. They managed the firm as it was, but didn't come up with new ideas how to expand or grow the firm. He didn't see any of them as a true leader. So, he decided to use a headhunter to find a new chief.

The headhunter firm identified Rupert Mason as a prime candidate. Mason headed a smaller similar firm in Texas. Mason's firm was growing at the rate of about 20% a year. Hendrix and Mason hit it off, and Hendrix was impressed with Mason's vision for Midway. Hendrix hired Mason to be the new CEO of Midway.

Before Mason accepted the offer, he asked Hendrix to get an undated resignation letter from each of the VPs. Mason wanted the opportunity to bring on his own leadership team, and he wanted that known before he took over, and wanted Hendrix to take the heat for this move. Hendrix was impressed with Mason's assertiveness and secured the resignation letters from the three VPs.

Mason came on board and took up his work. In the first six months he spent considerable time with the three VPs, individually and collectively. He found them friendly, competent, and managing their respective portfolios in an acceptable manner. Mason's family was welcomed into the fold and Mason's wife quickly made friends with the VPs' spouses. Mason settled in with his executive team.

In his heart Mason was not exactly satisfied with the work of three of the VPs. He didn't think they were aggressive enough in their leadership style. They weren't pushing their areas of the business in a way that would represent a breakthrough strategy. On the other hand, they were competent and seemed satisfied with the mid-level compensation level they were getting. Profits were still growing at about a 6% rate.

Mason investigated some other possibilities for the three positions, but he soon found that he would have to raise the compensation by about 50% to get the ideal leaders for the positions. He knew that if he could get the revenues and profits up another 10% the firm could easily afford the new compensation level, but the sticker price threw him off his game.

So, Mason kicked the can down the road and waited another three months to decide. After nine months on the job he concluded that things were going okay, so he chose not to make waves. He decided to keep the three VPs in place and move ahead with the mediocre growth rate. He left the mediocre VPs in place to do their management work, and left true leadership to be resolved sometime in the future. Mason settled for good folks, but ones not appropriate for their jobs.

Hendrix, watching from the side, was disappointed in this development, for Mason had not lived up to Hendrix' expectations.

Discussion Questions

1. Should Hendrix have had a claw-back provision to take back control of the firm?

2. Did Mason wait too long to make a decision about the three VPs?

3. Did Mason let his interpersonal relationships with the VPs affect his thinking about their competence in the job?

4. After a year, should Hendrix step in and try to give some advice to Mason?

5. Is it ever acceptable for a leader to allow for mediocrity in key management positions in a firm? Why or why not?

Analysis

This story represents a typical management failure for leaders who are afraid to make tough personnel decisions and who are risk adverse.

Mason waited too long to make the changes he really wanted. It was more comfortable to go with the existing gang, let them go on with their unexciting leadership, and not make waves. He compounded the problem by settling in with them at a family level. With his wife making friends of the other VP's wives, that made it more difficult to change them out.

Mason was not willing to take a risk and increase compensation needed to get higher quality VPs. Mason wanted to get the business humming, then make the change. He wasn't willing to see that the new and improved VPs would be the ones to bring in the new business and higher revenues. Making hard decisions is part of management.

Management takes courage and guts. Managers who are not willing to make tough decisions should reconsider their career path.

Case 3.21: Managing the Accountant

Rockwell Independent School District was located in the fast-growing town of Montel, Colorado. The school district had been adding new students each year for a number of years, but the administrative and operations departments were falling behind. They were struggling to keep up with the increased workload. The new Finance Director, Tanya Andrews, identified the need to hire an Accountant to help the Accounting Manager keep on top of the growing finances of the district. After posting the new Accountant position for a number of months, they received a couple of applications. All of the applicants were unqualified for the position, except one: Misty Evans.

Evans held a bachelor's degree in accounting from a reputable university, and she had some limited experience with hands-on accounting. Interestingly enough, during the first interview, Andrews learned that Evans had a pending lawsuit against her former employer. Nevertheless, Andrews felt the pressure to get the Accountant position filled, and since Evans was the only qualified candidate, Andrews went against her better judgment and offered her the position. She started the following week.

Over the next several months, Evans learned the responsibilities of her position, and the accounting practices of the school district. As time went on, she became more vocal about processes and procedures that she disagreed with. She brought many concerns up to Andrews, who took her complaints seriously and provided thoughtful responses to them. When

Andrews was unsure of a particular practice that Evans brought up, she would contact other accounting professionals to get their take on whether the process was adequate or not.

Over time, the complaints from Evans became exhausting. Evans even accused Andrews of not complying with state law regarding the accounting of voter-approved tax levy funds. Andrews took time to explain the state laws, and clearly pointed out the statutory authorities that allowed for the practice that was being performed. Evans went over Andrews' head and brought the complaints to the administration and the school board. Again, Evans' complaints were found baseless.

After some time had passed, a national recession ensued, which impacted funding of federal and state budgets. States were finding ways to slash their budgets, and in Colorado, one such cut was in funding for public schools. With Rockwell anticipating less revenue the following fiscal year, they had to make some tough decisions. One of the cost-savings measures identified by the Expense Reduction Task Force included the elimination of a position in the finance department. Andrews wanted to seek input from the managers in her department, and asked them to perform a thorough review of each position in the department and assess whether the position was critical or not. Throughout the process, the position that was identified as the least critical position in the department was the Accountant position that Evans occupied. Therefore, Andrews and her team agreed on a timeline and planned to let Evans know that due to budget constraints, her position was going to be eliminated. They intended to give Evans 30-days' notice, and they agreed that they would inform Evans the following week.

However, the day before Andrews was going to call Evans in and relay the bad news, Evans approached Andrews and shared some news with her - she was pregnant! Andrews felt awful. She felt so bad about laying off Evans since she was pregnant and would need the income to prepare for the baby. Furthermore, Andrews felt terrible that Evans would lose health insurance benefits at such a critical time. This also made Andrews very nervous about letting Evans go now, because all she could think about was that she would be accused of laying off Evans because she was pregnant. Andrews consulted with Rockwell's HR director, and they decided that they would keep Evans on board, wait for her to have her baby, give her the maternity leave she was entitled to, and upon her return, they would terminate her, in hopes of avoiding a wrongful termination lawsuit. They thought they could justify the termination by explaining that they realized how unneeded the position was because they got along just fine without it while Evans was out on maternity leave.

Several months later, Evans gave birth, and took eight weeks off for maternity leave. Upon return to work, Andrews decided to address the termination after a week or so. Andrews and the HR director met with Evans, and delivered the news of her position being eliminated. Evans seemed to take it in stride, and finished out the reminder of the week.

A short while later, Evans filed a lawsuit against the school district for wrongful termination. Evans claimed that in addition to being retaliated against for bringing poor accounting practices to the surface, she was also terminated because she took maternity leave. She was claiming protection under whistleblower laws as well as the Pregnancy Discrimination Act. After two years of litigation, the school district ended up settling the claim for a large sum of money.

Discussion Questions

1. Did Andrews check out Evans' lawsuit against her previous employer? Should that have raised a yellow if not a red flag about hiring Evans?

2. Why did Andrews go ahead and fill the new position with a second-tier candidate?

3. Why did Andrews let the situation go on so long with a disgruntled employee?

4. Should Andrews have told Evans in advance of the maternity leave that the position was going to be eliminated after the leave was finished?

5. Could Andrews have brought in an outside consulting firm to determine which job or jobs to eliminate, and thus taken some of the heat off of Andrews and her administration?

Analysis

Andrews dug a grave for herself by hiring Evans. She evidently didn't do her homework in checking with Evans' previous employer, for she got in a hurry to fill this new position.

There was no real need for Andrews to be in such a hurry. The district had gotten by without the position, so it could go a few more months without the new position being filled; Andrews needed more patience.

Andrews got into a real bind. By failing to act earlier about Evans' place in the firm and Evans' failure to become a good employee, Andrews now had to face a maternity leave just at the time she decided to act on Evans' position.

The school district did its own study on which positions to eliminate. It opened itself up to accusations of bias and discrimination. It could have used an outside management consulting firm to do the study and make the recommendations on the position or positions to eliminate.

The School Board had already acted on Evans' claims about poor accounting practices, so that claim should have been easily rebutted. Administrative records should have shown that the decision to eliminate the position was made before Evans informed Andrews that she was pregnant, so Evans' claim under the Pregnancy Discrimination Act should have been fairly easy to refute. All in all, the School Board should have taken this to public court and fought the case rather than giving a large settlement to Evans.

Case 3.22: The Great Divide

Dayton Production of Dayton, Ohio was a company built and sold bicycles. It was one of the few bicycle manufacturers left in the United States; most other bicycle companies had migrated off shore. Dayton Production introduced lean manufacturing soon after Japanese industries went lean and automated early. Dayton's gross revenues ran in the $70M range. Principal customers were the big-box chains as well as several traditional retailers.

Dayton's assembly plant was in Dayton, as was the product design office. Dayton had sales offices in New York, Atlanta, Chicago, Denver, and San Francisco. Sales personnel regularly called on Dayton's customers as well as potential customers in their territories. These personnel had considerable freedom in signing contracts with customers. Sales personnel were compensated on a percentage of sale price basis.

Dayton's sales personnel were very similar in their personalities, drive, and passion for the product. They pushed the bicycles aggressively and continually signed new sales contracts. However, that got them in trouble with the production people back home. The sales personnel would make commitments which were outside the range of normal production. Especially grievous were fast time commitments on orders. These commitments would give the production people a great deal of heartburn, causing them to add shifts, pay overtime, and work harder. The additional costs also cut down on profits. In sum, there was a constant battle between the sales and production folks.

The sales personnel were always trying to get sales, but regularly complained to the folks back in the main office that the products were not up to snuff. Sales wanted new products, new designs, and new materials. They felt thwarted in their sales efforts because they didn't have the best and brightest to sell. They were always reporting to central management about the failure of the design team to keep up with new developments.

The design folks reciprocated with bad attitudes toward the sales folks. The design folks thought the design office was keeping up with the new technologies, the new designs, and the new materials. Sales were good, so why should the sales folks complain?

So, Dayton experienced the cultural divide that occurs so often in production/sales companies: the great three-way war between sales, product development, and production.

Discussion Questions

1. How can Dayton's management align these three cultures so they are not fighting against each other?

2. Can Dayton's management set up an information flow system that helps the three groups keep better synchronized with each other?

3. Do the leaders of the three groups have regular

communication with each other?

4. How can companies prevent similar cultural divides among different departments?

5. What role does a manager play in shaping and forming an organization's culture?

Analysis

Dayton's problems are similar to those in other build and sell organizations. It seems to come with the territory; the three groups march to different drummers and each is constantly blaming the other two for holding it back.

The product development people want to have the freedom to develop the new products at their own pace. They believe they are keeping up with technological and social trends; the other two groups don't have a good handle on what is happening in the marketplace.

The sales people want to sell more product; that's what their compensation is tied to. If the product is not available to give to prospective buyers, then sales are curtailed, as is their paychecks. In their dream world there would be an infinite supply of the latest and best product available on the market, at a price that would sell to the public.

The production people are in a bind. They are restricted by physics, engineering, technology, facilities, and the raw materials and production equipment on hand. They would like to build enough product to meet the needs of the sales people, but if the salespeople sell too much and make unwise time commitments to the buyers, it leaves the production people in a jam.

One way these problems can be diminished is to assure there is good communication among the three areas. The leaders should be meeting regularly and sharing information about developments, production, and sales. Each group should be making good projections about its future work so the other two groups will know what is coming in the near future and as far out as possible. Senior management should make sure the three groups are working together as much as possible.

It doesn't hurt to get together the workers from the three areas. Have company social events so they can get acquainted with each other and try to build some personal relationships. Encourage some cross training and job sharing so that workers can begin to understand the challenges and opportunities available to people in the other groups.

Case 3.23: Too Big a Span

Betty Cartwright was the Chief Operating Officer (COO) of the Texas Manufacturing Corporation, a $50M company in Abilene, Texas. Cartwright reported directly to the CEO, and five division heads reported to Cartwright. Below the division heads were 31 departments, each headed by a department head.

The CEO and Cartwright were watching the company's growth and concluded that the firm was not growing as fast as it should. Further, Cartwright decided that her five-division head direct reports were not as aggressive and committed as they should be. So, Cartwright decided to reorganize her management structure by eliminating the five divisions and reducing the number of departments to 27. Further, each of the department heads would report directly to her. Cartwright's office staff had five people, each of which reported directly to her, so in this new structure Cartwright had 32 direct reports.

The restructuring caused considerable heartburn, especially among the five division heads. Three left the company, while two remained and were given department head positions when two department heads retired.

Cartwright had a management philosophy that she would have at least one meeting a week with each of her 27 principal direct reports, so she had her assistant set up a permanent meeting schedule of 27 half-hour meetings with those 27 people. Since the former divisions remained as a shadow structure, Cartwright had group meetings with the department heads from each of the former divisions.

Cartwright had been promoted to the COO position from one of the former division heads, so she was quite knowledgeable about the work of the four departments that were in the division she formerly led. But it took Cartwright six months to get up to speed with each of the 23 other departments.

After a few months she started to get complaints from some of the department heads. It was claimed that she wasn't giving enough attention to some of the departments. Several complained about the weekly meetings as generally being nonproductive. A few complained because Cartwright didn't keep a strict control of her meetings and often meetings would run over the scheduled time, causing personnel to cool their heels waiting for Cartwright to be ready to meet.

After a year with the new structure, Cartwright was exhausted. Her meeting schedule was so heavy during work hours that she couldn't get all her COO work done. She would typically take work home, and spend three to four hours per night trying to get caught up.

After 18 months in the new structure, Cartwright pulled the plug. She recognized, as did the CEO, that the structure was not working; Cartwright had too many direct reports. Cartwright then proposed, and the CEO accepted, that the firm return to the previous structure, this time with seven divisions. The new structure was implemented and Cartwright's life returned to some degree of normality.

Discussion Questions

1. Cartwright had a philosophy about meeting with her direct reports each week and for one-half hour. Was that a good management approach?

2. Cartwright apparently didn't have a philosophy about the number of direct reports she could handle. In general, what is a good range of direct reports one manager can handle?

3. What are the factors that determine how many direct reports one manager can handle?

4. Should Cartwright have solicited input from other leaders in the organization before pulling the trigger on the reorganization?

5. What impacts does a significant reorganization like this have on company leaders? Employees? Customers?

Analysis

Underlying Cartwright's management philosophy was the belief that she had to be close to the work and in control. This attitude manifested itself in her desire to meet for a half-hour each week with each of her direct reports. Cartwright wanted to know in depth what was going on.

She also wanted a broad span of control; lots of people reporting directly to her. Adding these two together, too much of Cartwright's time was spent talking to her subordinates. She should have given each of them more authority to work his or her area of responsibility without having to report every detail to Cartwright.

Cartwright took way too long to determine her new structure was not working. She should have been able to realize her trouble within six months at most. After a year she then waited another six months before making an adjustment in the structure.

While senior executives typically work 60-80 hours a week, Cartwright's added responsibilities resulted in another 20 hours a week on the average. That added work contributed to difficulties at home; Cartwright's husband complained about a breakdown in their marriage. The complaints of the husband should have been a wake-up call to Cartwright that something needed to change, and another solution to the reporting structure was warranted.

Case 3.24: Watch Your Elasticity

Joseph Billings was the owner and manager of Stallion Automobile Company, an automobile sales and service company located in Salt Lake City, Utah. Billings started Stallion after being discharged from the Army following the Korean War. Stallion was the typical auto sales company, selling new and used cars and making considerable money from its auto service center.

In 2014 Stallion sold 278 new cars, with a gross revenue of $8,773,680 (net of trade-ins). The average net per new car sold was $31,560. Billings felt good about the sales, but thought he could do better.

Billings devised a plan to sell more cars. He said he would cut the average cost of new cars by 10%, and he expected to get a 20% boost in sales. He did not do a market study to arrive at the 20% figure; rather, he projected based on his own understanding of the market. He calculated the average net revenue per new car sold would be $28,404, the number of new cars sold would be 333 and the total net revenue from new car sales would be $9,458.532, which would be a 7.8% increase in total net revenues from new car sales. The dollar increase would be $684,852.

Billings liked his plan, so he went to work and implemented it. During 2015 he spent an extra $87,000 in advertising, hired three additional mechanics in the service shop, brought on two new car salespersons, and waited for the sales to come in.

Unfortunately for Billings, reality didn't follow his dreams. By the end of 2015 the number of new cars sold increased from 278 to 302. The average selling price was $28,526 (net of trade-ins), bringing in a total net revenue of $8,614,852, which was actually $158,828 less than the revenues brought in in 2014. Adding the costs of the salespersons and additional advertising, Billings' profit in 2015 for the sales division were approximately $200,000 less than in 2014.

After the books closed for 2015, Billings decided he had made a mistake in cutting prices, so he started to raise prices up to what he viewed as normal. He raised prices by 5% in 2016, which resulted in his selling only 295 cars, for a total net revenue of $8,835,840. In 2017 he raised prices by another 5% and sold 302 new cars, for a total revenue of $9,497,598. By then Billings thought he was back on track with his prices and sales.

Discussion Questions

1. Why did Billings think he was going to get a 20% increase in sales after making the reduction in price? Did he do a market study? What type of study would you suggest for this scenario?

2. What was happening to car sales at the local, state, and national levels? Should Billings have taken that into consideration when making his sales projections?

3. Should Billings have gone ahead with hiring the additional personnel before the new sales numbers came in?

4. What methods of accountability could be put in

place for visionary plans such as Billings'?

5. What is meant by elasticity?

Analysis

Billings apparently didn't know about the concept of elasticity, although he did perform calculations that would have been called for in an elasticity study. He projected a 20% increase in sales, without evidence so far as we know.

He was very sure of his projection. In fact, he was so sure that he put additional staff members on the payroll before the surge in sales was to come in. He added fixed cost, and expected new income to be generated.

After Billings decided he had been wrong, he tried to recover on his sales price, starting out with reduced prices and trying to build back up to where he was before he made the cuts. Now he found himself having to raise prices faster than he otherwise would have done, and that wouldn't set well with potential customers.

If there was one thing that Billings did wrong, it probably was his failure to do a market study.

Case 3.25: That's Not the Way We Do Things

Dax Mayfield was the operations manager for his firm, a medical supply company. Mayfield had six direct reports. Mayfield had good relationships with his direct reports, both professionally and personally. Mayfield was in his position for six years, and each direct report had at least four years of experience with the company.

On one occasion, Mary Rand, one of Mayfield's direct reports and head of the manufacturing division, met with Mayfield in a regular bi-weekly meeting. After exchanging small talk, they entered into a discussion about Rand's section and various topics related to product development. In the discussion Rand asked for authorization to purchase a new five-axle lathe which, she claimed, would pay for itself in two years. The purchase price was good, but would hold for only two more days. Mayfield remembered that in the past requests for major purchases of the type Rand wanted would go to a management committee for discussion, although Mayfield made the final decision. Mayfield told Rand, "We can't do that because we've never done it that way before."

As soon as Mayfield made the statement he knew he was in trouble with Rand. Both Rand and Mayfield saw immediately that the reason given didn't make any management sense. Both started to laugh and Rand gave Mayfield a hard time for being so ridiculous.

To dig himself out of the hole he was in, Mayfield said, "Go ahead. It's a good idea you have and I know no reason why it wouldn't be productive for the firm. Do it!

Rand left the meeting happy, and Mayfield learned that the reason to not take a course of action such as "We haven't done it that way before" was not going to fly. A good lesson learned.

Discussion Questions

1. Is "that's not the way we do things around here" ever an acceptable response to an organizational issue?

2. Was there another way for Mayfield to recover from the embarrassment of giving a poor reason for not approving Rand's request?

3. Did Mayfield do the right thing by approving the purchase without taking it to the management committee?

4. If he didn't want to take it to the management committee, should Mayfield have done his own analysis of Rand's proposal?

5. Mayfield could be perceived by the management team as going rogue on this decision. What are some possible ramifications of this?

Analysis

Mayfield in the middle of the conversation gave an inadequate response to a legitimate request. He immediately knew his response was ill-formed.

There seems to have been good rapport between Mayfield and Rand, so he might have apologized for the mistaken response and gone on from there.

We don't know the culture of the organization. We don't know if the other managers would be alarmed that Mayfield allowed the expenditure to move forward without more review by the committee. Had this happened before? Was Mayfield in such a strong position politically that he didn't care what the members of the committee thought?

If Mayfield ran into trouble with his committee, he didn't have much to stand on. He didn't conduct his own analysis of the situation. He didn't check Rand's figures about cost recovery. He didn't check to see if the purchase price was good.

Mayfield was put in a box by Rand. She wanted a decision immediately so the firm could take advantage of what she viewed as a good deal. Rand was squeezed to make a quick decision, and made it off the top of his head.

Hopefully the good Rand predicted turned out to be the case. If not, Mayfield would have egg on his face.

Case 3.26: Something Smells

One evening a family of four went out to eat at a local Italian restaurant. A few minutes after being seated, a waiter came to the table and welcomed the family to the restaurant. He also asked to take their drink order. The family thought that something seemed weird about the waiter. His speech was a bit slurred, and he was walking a bit unevenly. Shortly thereafter, two young women were seated at the booth across from the family. The waiter immediately attended to the women, and began engaging in conversation with them for an extended period of time.

The family, waiting for their drinks, observed that the waiter was laughing and carrying on quite a conversation with the women. After some time, the waiter left, and returned with the family's drinks. The waiter told the family that he would be right back to take their meal order. The waiter proceeded to visit the table with the two women, once again laughing and talking with them for an extended period of time. Finally, the waiter came to take the family's order. The waiter still seemed to be off, as he kept on asking the family to repeat their order and seemed to struggle to write the order legibly.

Finally, the order was complete, and the waiter went to the kitchen to enter the order. Soon thereafter, he returned to the table with the two young women, and continued his conversation and laughter. Soon thereafter, a manager walked by the family, and so the family explained the situation to the manager.

After the family explained the situation to the manager, the manager went over to the waiter, pulled him aside, and had a conversation with him. Upon the conclusion of the conversation, the waiter went back to the kitchen to check on the family's meal. In the meantime, the manager came back to the family and apologized for the waiter's behavior. The manager indicated to the family that he believed that the waiter was intoxicated – that he had been drinking prior to his shift. The family agreed that the explanation would be consistent with the behavior they observed. In light of this, the manager did nothing. The waiter continued to work, and the family continued to receive sub-par service for the remainder of the night.

Discussion Questions

1. Did the manager handle this situation effectively?

2. Why didn't the manager remove the intoxicated waiter from service?

3. Why did the manager tell the customers what the problem was with the waiter?

4. What could the manager have done to turn the family into delighted customers?

5. How can managers better ensure that employees are providing high levels of customer service without micromanaging?

Analysis

The waiter was clearly in the wrong. The waiter was intoxicated and couldn't carry out his duties adequately. The waiter was also out of line by spending so much time chatting up one table of guests and neglecting other guests.

The manager was clearly not on top of this situation. It appears that the waiter had not been trained. It appears the waiter was allowed to come to work intoxicated. The manager should have been aware of the situation before the problem hit the customers.

The manager could have reassigned the table to another waiter, or taken care of the table him- or herself, then begin the work of turning the visit into a delightful one for the customers. If necessary, the meal could have been provided for free.

The manager did not need to tell the customers what the problem was with the waiter. The manager should have worked with the waiter behind closed doors and relieved the waiter of duty until the waiter was sober. Then a retraining session should have been given to the waiter to attempt to bring him up to speed. If there had been other incidents, the manager might have needed to let the waiter go away permanently.

Case 3.27: The Wishy-Washy CEO

Tuscaloosa Productions, Inc. was a $100M firm in Alabama. It was a 75-year-old manufacturing firm that built custom-made steel products. Its long-term CEO (25-year tenure) announced his retirement and a search was conducted for a successor.

The finalist list included four candidates. Two were from the West Coast, one was from the Midwest, and one was the current Senior Vice President. The search committee soon eliminated the two candidates from the West Coast. The internal candidate had been in the firm for two decades and over that time had built up a group of supporters and a group of detractors. The search committee eventually decided not to go with the internal candidate and recommended that the Board hire the man from the Midwest. They left the Senior Vice President in place as the Executive Vice President.

The new CEO was a gregarious man who meshed well with Tuscaloosa Productions' mission. He had previous experience in a similar company in Illinois, and knew the steel production business very well. He was a family man with a very talented wife and three exceptional children. It was evident that he took great pride in his family. He had been born in Germany and lived there until he came to the United States for college; he was fluent in German.

So, we had in place a CEO (President) and Executive Vice President (EVP) who had both applied for the CEO job. The two individuals couldn't have been more different. The EVP was a man used to making decisions; he was decisive and didn't take a long time to make decisions - even big and difficult decisions. The CEO, on the other hand, was indecisive. He believed in consensus management. He called on his C-team colleagues to help him make decisions. If there was not near unanimity among the C-group, he would postpone a decision until more discussion had taken place. He tended to agree with whoever talked to him last about a problem. Also, he seemed to depend a lot on the advice of the EVP.

The EVP was not a supporter of the CEO. In private conversation with others he would trash the CEO and make fun of his management style and decisions. In public they were quite civil to each other. One suspects that the CEO never knew what the EVP was thinking and saying behind the CEO's back.

Most of the new thrusts over the CEO's 11-year tenure came from the EVP. The CEO continued to be the public front for the firm, but seemed inadequate to propose breakthrough strategies to move the firm ahead.

Eventually the Board of Directors woke up to the CEO's management style and lack of decisive leadership. The Board hired an outside consultant to study the CEO's work and make a recommendation about his continuation in office. As a result of the study the CEO was kept on as CEO, but his duties were restricted to public representation of the firm. The EVP was appointed as internal president and effectively ran the organization. That structure lasted about six months when the CEO resigned and left town. The EVP was then named as Acting CEO until further arrangements could be made. After some consideration, the Board appointed the Acting CEO to the CEO spot permanently.

Discussion Questions

1. Should the Board have done more homework to investigate the CEO's management style prior to onboarding him?

2. Should the Board have left the EVP in position when he failed to be appointed as CEO?

3. What are the ethical implications of the EVP trash-talking behind the CEO's back? What are the implications for the organization's culture?

4. How could the CEO have determined what the EVP was saying and doing about the CEO and the CEO's work?

5. Could the other direct reports of the CEO have alerted him to the EVP's lack of respect for the CEO?

Analysis

The Board made a serious mistake when it left in place the runner-up for the CEO position. The man who got the position came in having to work with the man who wanted his job. The new CEO should have requested the EVP's resignation before accepting the CEO spot.

The EVP had serious ethical deficiencies. By publicly

denigrating the CEO he undermined the effectiveness of the CEO and set the CEO for failure downstream.

The Board never investigated the management style of their new CEO. The CEO's consensus management style was good for peacetime, but couldn't effectively handle crises or urgent matters. The firm's forward momentum was thwarted because of the lack of decisiveness of the CEO.

To the rest of the employees of the firm, the stark difference between the management styles of the CEO and the EVP made for many snide comments and disruption in day-to-day work.

The Board appears to have been a pass-through board, which didn't take action on the executive suite until matters got really bad. Then their solution was to continue both the CEO and the EVP in place, but change their job descriptions. The CEO soon saw this was an unworkable situation, and left.

This cleared the way for the Board to appoint the EVP as the new CEO.

Case 3.28: You've Got to Care, But Not That Much!

Paul Coffman was the President and CEO of a century-old company that marketed and sold self-improvement products. The company, Southwest Services, Inc. of South Carolina, was successful to a degree but had plateaued and seemed no longer to be growing. Coffman became committed to the concept of restoring growth in the future. He announced to all of his management team that the number one strategic goal of the company needed to be restored growth with the ultimate aim of increasing revenue.

After some discussion within the management team, Coffman became convinced that the primary problem that was preventing Southwest's growth was an outdated marketing strategy. Coffman had studied successful competitors and determined that Southwest needed to make a major commitment to online marketing, using the internet and social media as a platform for finding and securing customers. Unfortunately, Southwest had no internal expertise and so Coffman was determined to find an external partner to undertake a new online marketing strategy.

Coffman talked to some colleagues in the industry, and finally settled on Spokesman Communication, Inc., an online marketing company that was a subsidiary of CommPartners of Florida. CommPartners was a publicly traded company listed on the NYSE. It was also true that CommPartners had experienced recent bad publicity concerning possible mismanagement (which was, of course, denied by CommPartners).

Spokesman was not a large company; it was relatively new (as was the science and art of online marketing). Spokesman did not have a lot of clients or references, but Coffman was told by one trusted colleague that this would be the best choice.

Coffman dispatched his COO, Brian Masters, and his General Counsel, Thomas Shellman, to the Spokesman offices in Atlanta to begin to flesh out a deal by which Spokesman would assume responsibility for Marketing Southwest products online. In the early discussions, Spokesman indicated that in order to take on the assignment it would require a fee of $2M per year (plus commissions for success) with a five-year contractual commitment. Spokesman argued that its primary costs were up front, and so the five-year commitment was needed to allow it to recover its investment and make a profit. Coffman and his team believed this to be a very large commitment for Southwest, but he was willing to pay the price to break into the online marketing game.

Once in Atlanta, the Southwest team met with senior management from Spokesman. They also included, by conference call, the General Counsel for CommPartners who was at the time in Boston.

As the discussion progressed, Southwest General Counsel Shellman, began to discuss various items of due diligence that Southwest would want to undertake. He met immediate resistance from the lawyer for CommPartners. Shellman pointed to the adverse publicity surrounding CommPartners and indicated that Southwest needed to assure itself that there was no problem that would interfere with the execution and performance of any contract. He also indicated a need to be sure that Spokesman had the wherewithal to perform the tasks that it was promising to do. The CommPartners lawyer flatly refused to allow any due diligence whatsoever. Masters and Shellman left the meeting in Atlanta with this issue unresolved.

Upon returning to the Southwest offices, Masters and Shellman found that Spokesman had transmitted a draft agreement. Shellman examined the proposed draft and found that the terms in the draft were wholly one-sided and were neither legally safe nor secure from Southwest's perspective. No accountability terms were included to ensure Spokesman's performance. Spokesman had dozens of ways to terminate the contract, but the agreement afforded Southwest no way out. Additional fees had been added, small but potentially significant in total. And when Shellman tried to negotiate these points, Spokesman, acting through the parent company's general counsel, refused to negotiate, asserting that the contract was "take it or leave it."

Shellman advised Coffman that from a legal perspective the terms of the proposed agreement were unsafe and could bind Southwest to five years of $2M payments without any assurance whatsoever that Spokesman would produce any beneficial results for Southwest. He told Coffman that in the event of a Spokesman failure, Southwest would still be on the hook for the full payment amount. He advised Coffman to walk away based on the refusal of CommPartners and Spokesman to allow due diligence and based on the one-sided and bad faith terms of the Agreement.

Coffman was committed to online marketing, and he could see no other alternative that could be implemented in a timely and effective way. He told his team that he was going forward with the one-sided deal notwithstanding legal counsel that he should not do so. At that point, Shellman gave him a written memo advising against the transaction. Masters agreed with Shellman but recognized Coffman's commitment and so remained quiet.

Within the first year of the contract (and with $2M already paid out) it became clear to everybody that Spokesman was producing no results and would likely not ever produce results. It was also clear that they were not investing as promised, and that the effort on Southwest's behalf was minimal. By the eighteen-month mark, Coffman had to reluctantly agree that Southwest needed to get out of the contract. There was no contractual basis for exiting the deal (as Shellman had warned) and so Southwest simply breached the contract and refused to pay more. Several years of expensive litigation followed, and the matter was eventually settled for several millions of dollars. In the end, Southwest could not identify any real benefit that it had derived from the contract.

Discussion Questions

1. How should a senior executive balance advice of legal counsel versus the operational needs of the company?

2. Would it have benefitted Coffman to "walk away" from Spokesman and see if a more advantageous deal might have been agreed to?

3. Was Shellman's demand for due diligence reasonable? Was it common or best practice?

4. Did Coffman become too convinced of the need for this particular deal? How can an executive avoid becoming so invested in a possible deal that he cannot walk away if the deal begins to look dangerous?

5. Do you perceive any ethical or moral issue with a decision to simply "breach" an unfavorable contract?

Analysis

Master Negotiator Herb Cohen, author of the best-selling book "You Can Negotiate Anything," once said that in any negotiation, you "need to care, but not t-h-a-t much!" Cohen recognized that it is not uncommon for an executive to seek out some result for the best of reasons, but to become so emotionally involved in the outcome the he or she loses perspective and so steps into the proverbial mud puddle.

Coffman was no doubt accurate in determining that Southwest required an updated marketing strategy. He was also undoubtedly correct that the new strategy needed to take advantage of new technology and new communication channels of online and through social media. In the fast-changing world of communication and marketing, it is easy to fall behind, and Coffman was probably right to settle on this approach.

And, he was probably right to seek out the counsel of colleagues in the industry and to trust their input. At that point in the process, he most certainly felt comfortable that he had charted the optimal course for Southwest.

The first red flag went up when CommPartners refused to allow due diligence of themselves or Spokesman. Due diligence is a normal part of any business transaction, particularly a large-dollar, long term arrangement. Denial of due diligence access certainly signals that the party refusing due diligence may be hiding something. In a real sense, Coffman should have walked away at that point, at least to see if they changed their position and perhaps permanently. But Coffman was too committed to accept this clear signal.

The second and dispositive red flag came with the one-sided proposed contract, and the refusal to negotiate. At this point, Coffman should have seen what the long-term relationship would feel like: one-sided. Again, he was too committed.

One safeguard against an adverse business transaction is the company's legal counsel. In this case, Shellman advised Coffman that the contract was a bad mistake, and went so far as to make a record of his advice in writing. Again, Coffman was too committed. Furthermore, Coffman undervalued the role of his counsel's advice because he was fixated on a desire to achieve hoped-for business results.

It's easy to get so committed to a course of action that you fail to see the pitfalls, even when your legal counsel is telling you no. As Herb Cohen says, you gotta care, but not t-h-a-t much!

This page intentionally left blank

CHAPTER FOUR

CASE STUDIES OF MANAGEMENT FAILURE

Not-for-Profit Firms

This page intentionally left blank

Case 4.1: Amorous Relationship II

Dr. Charlotte Wilson was the Chair of the Political Science Department at Sheldon University in Texas. The department had eight professors including Wilson. Wilson had been chair of the department for nine years, did a good job, and was liked by her immediate superior, the Dean of the College of Liberal Studies, Dr. Kevin Smith.

One of the other professors in the Political Science Department was Dr. David Keff. Keff's specialization was Constitutional Law. Keff was one of the department's professors most popular with the students. Keff was tall, very handsome, and very muscular. Keff had been at the university for 12 years.

Wilson liked Keff. He was quite cooperative with Wilson's direction of the department. Keff supported Wilson in almost all her decisions. Over time Wilson appointed Keff to significant committees. Wilson gave strong support for Keff's promotions and tenure.

Wilson typically attended five professional conferences each year, three having to do with political science and two having to do with university administration. Keff typically attended two professional meetings a year, the two being ones that Wilson also attended. At the conferences they attended together they would pal around, eat meals together, and usually attended one or two cultural events in the convention cities.

On one trip after an evening meal together, Wilson invited Keff to her hotel room. While there Wilson began to kiss Keff which ended up with the two of them in bed. That evening's tryst started a two-year affair between Wilson and Keff.

One of the problems in the relationship was that Keff was already married. His wife and two children at home did not know of Keff's relationship with Wilson, although the wife thought there was some cooling in their marriage relationship.

Dean Smith noticed the close relationship developing between Wilson and Keff. Two staff members also informally commented to Smith about the situation. However, Smith took no action because of his previous good relationship with Wilson and his belief in her good work and integrity.

After two years of the affair, Keff's wife accused Keff of having an affair and he confessed his relationship with Wilson. Keff promised his wife he would break off the affair, which he did.

Wilson was distraught. She thought Keff would divorce his wife and marry her. She broke her good fellowship with Keff and started to demean him in department meetings. The new atmosphere drove Keff to lodge a complaint against Wilson, and accuse her of sexual harassment and abuse.

The complaint went to the university's HR department and to Dean Smith. After due investigation, both Wilson and Keff were given formal reprimands and Wilson was removed as Chair of the Department of Political Science. The information about the affair leaked, with the department's professors taking sides between Wilson and Keff. Relationships in the department were strained thereafter. After two years Wilson left Sheldon University to take a professorship at New Mexico Women's University.

Discussion Questions

1. What should Dean Smith have done when he noticed a very close relationship emerging between Wilson and Keff?

2. What should Wilson have done to protect herself from the bad situation which emerged?

3. What should Keff have done to protect himself from the bad situation which emerged?

4. What policies should the university put in place to inhibit situations of this type?

5. Should Sheldon University institute an Amorous Relationship Policy?

Analysis

Both Wilson and Keff had a moral lapse. Keff allowed himself to get into a situation in which he yielded to temptation to become intimate with Wilson. Not only was Wilson out of line in paying too much attention to Keff but carrying it further into the bedroom. Wilson grossly erred in having a sexual relationship with a subordinate, opening herself up to charges of sexual harassment.

Smith was blinded by his years of good work with

Wilson. He did not investigate and take action when it was clear that Wilson and Keff were getting too close to each other.

The story describes the fall-out of this bad situation. Both Wilson and Keff got formal reprimands. Wilson lost her job as chair of the department. Faculty in the department took sides between Wilson and Keff, with much loss of morale in the department. After five years there were still bad feelings among several of the department's faculty. Smith continued on as Dean, but that incident soured Smith's upline Vice President, who passed over Dean when bringing in a new Associate Vice President.

Case 4.2: Appearances Matter

Peter Edmunds was a CPA. He started his career at a Big Six accounting firm. One of his larger clients was a chemical company, Cascadia Chemical and Substances, Inc. Cascadia was a successful company listed on the NYSE. Edmunds worked on Cascadia audits. He was congenial and friendly, but also highly skilled and effective. The management team at Cascadia noticed Edmunds, became friends, and after several years the company decided to offer Edmunds a job in-house as their controller. Edmunds was successful as a controller, and eventually, when the position opened, he was elevated to serve as Chief Financial Officer.

While Edmunds was CFO of Cascadia, the company was the subject of a tender offer and the controlling interest in the company was purchased by a British venture capitalist. The British venture capitalist assumed the position of CEO. It did not take long for Edmunds and the Board of Directors to recognize that there were noteworthy differences between the ethical standards of the British venture capitalist and ethical and legal standards in the United States.

The chemical sector can be volatile and there came a time when the financial success of Cascadia began to wane. At the same time, it became clear that the British CEO had engaged in significant self-dealing. The Board of Directors then terminated the employment of the British CEO for cause and asked Edmunds to assume the position of CEO.

Edmunds began to reorganize the executive suite.

He brought on a new General Counsel, David Latham, who had previously worked for a subsidiary of Cascadia. Edmunds had worked with Latham while he was CFO and Latham had served at the subsidiary. The two had a strong and trusting relationship.

As the financial condition continued to deteriorate at Cascadia, it became clear that a Chapter Eleven Bankruptcy would be the only strategy that might allow for the continuation of the Cascadia story. During this time everybody on the management team worked long hours, often into the evening. It was not unusual for management team members, including Edmunds and Latham, to work until 10:00 pm.

Edmunds had an administrative assistant named Suzanna. Suzanna was educated, skilled, hard-working, kept confidences, and was all-in-all a superb administrative assistant. There was no doubt that Edmunds and Suzanna worked well together. They communicated well and constantly. It was not uncommon to see Suzanna standing behind Edmunds' desk, looking over his shoulder at his computer or leaning over his desk while examining some document of draft. They shared a sense of humor, even under stress, and often laughed at some joke or amusing condition.

As the bankruptcy process advanced, and the operational needs of the company continued to be demanding, Edmunds worked longer and longer hours, often staying well after the other management team members headed home, and often arriving earlier than the other team members. And when Edmunds was at the office, Suzanna was also at the office.

Many who worked with the management team, including team members, outside counsel, and members of the Board of Directors, started to notice the relationship between Edmunds and Suzanna. Rumors began to circulate. Both Edmunds and Suzanna were married, and both had children. The notion that there was a romantic relationship became a common assumption. In fact, there was no romantic involvement, but those associated with the company would not believe that to be true.

Eventually, the rumors of the affair reached the creditors and their attorneys, who were active in the bankruptcy. When he learned that the creditors were talking about the purported relationship, Latham decided that it was time to take action for the good of the company. Latham recognized that the rumor (notwithstanding reality) could be harmful to Cascadia in the Bankruptcy.

Latham arranged a meeting with Edmunds outside of the company offices. He advised Edmunds of the appearance of an affair, of the rumors, and of the potential harm. He advised Edmunds to expect questions about the purported affair, and the mounting evidence of its existence, in an upcoming deposition in the Bankruptcy proceeding.

At first Edmunds denied that there was any problem. In a short time, however, he came to realize that the appearance was real. Unfortunately, it was too late. The creditors took action in the bankruptcy proceeding to replace Edmunds (and Suzanna). They argued that the affair was distracting Edmunds and that the result would be harmful to the creditors. The Bankruptcy Judge took the matter under advisement. In the end, one major creditor obtained control of the company by way of the bankruptcy, and both Edmunds and Suzanna were terminated.

Discussion Questions

1. Did the financial condition of the company and the bankruptcy contribute to the conditions that resulted in an appearance of impropriety? What might have been done to alleviate the pressures that contributed to the problem?

2. Does an appearance of impropriety really matter if there was no real romantic involvement?

3. Assume that Edmunds did need to work unreasonably long hours and assume that he did need administrative support during all the hours that he was working. How can a manager maintain situational awareness and avoid the sort of misunderstanding that occurred here?

4. Was the "intervention" undertaken by Latham with regard to Edmunds conduct solely the responsibility of the General Counsel, or should other members of the management team or the Board also have stepped up, perhaps even earlier? Why might those others not have acted to advise Edmunds?

5. Why would the creditors of Cascadia be concerned about the rumors of an affair between the company CEO and his administrative assistant?

Analysis

In the business world appearances can be as important as reality. Minor actions, no matter how justified they may be, are likely to be noticed (often by those who fit the phrase "none of your business") and misconstrued. And adversity can follow.

Edmunds and Suzanna were obviously both pleasant and competent, and they were a good fit from a business performance point of view. It was actually that fit that helped foster the rumors and misunderstandings. In the business world (the executive suite or elsewhere) a relationship between two persons (particularly one that has the potential for a romantic element) that is very close and connected can and will be easily assigned the title of "affair."

As the company suffered economic decline and entered the Chapter Eleven Bankruptcy, the workload in the executive suite doubled. The management team had to manage both the ongoing business of Cascadia and the bankruptcy proceeding and all of its demands. Money was tight, so the option of hiring more team members to take up the load was not available. So, everybody worked harder and longer. And stress mounted. It was entirely appropriate for both Edmunds and Suzanna to work both early and late, but the fact that they might have been alone together at odd hours was fertile ground for misunderstanding and adverse assumptions. What often happens in such a situation is that the two involved are too close to the situation to see what others see.

The stress of the bankruptcy also reached to the creditors who stood to lose a lot of money. They expected Edmunds to be focused on the financial health of the company, and feared that he was being distracted by a romantic liaison was something that was reasonable from their perspective.

The business sins in this case were sins of omission. Everybody, including Edmunds, Suzanna, Latham, the rest of the executive team, and Board of Directors, needed to be aware, wary, and reactive. The best solution in this case was for somebody, optimally Edmunds, to recognize the risk of misperception, and to stop the perception from the start. While Edmunds needed more self-awareness, something that could be difficult under the stressful demands of the context, all of the others should have been free to do what Latham did, and perhaps earlier, without fear of any retribution from Edmunds. Edmunds would have been well served to create an atmosphere of trust where anybody could have come to him and told him to avoid situations where he and Suzanna were alone.

In other words, it was not enough for Edmunds to know that he was not misbehaving. He needed to be more self-aware. And he needed to avoid situations which might give rise to a naughty rumor. Situational awareness is key for managers. After all, appearances are often as powerful, or perhaps even more powerful, than reality.

Case 4.3: Don't Bust Your Budget

It's easy to go off the rails in managing the budget. Your revenues may tank. A catastrophe may occur that shuts your operations down for a few weeks. The CEO may get killed in a plane wreck and key investor information goes to the grave with her. The government may impose new regulations that kill your expense budget.

Then there's just common run-of-the-mill mismanagement. That happened to Cherokee Enterprises, a not-for-profit organization in Virginia. Cherokee was a small service group that provided personal services to physically handicapped people in the Roanoke area. Cherokee's total annual revenues were in the $20M range.

Cherokee got a new CEO who had a vision for a bigger service impact. He decided to go all out and add services, enhance Cherokee's facilities, and do a better job of marketing. With his management team, and with the approval of the board, he developed a $25M revenue budget and a $25M expense budget.

Cherokee embarked on a new fiscal year with excitement. With the added dollars in marketing, Cherokee got a lot of press and publicity in the Roanoke area. There were many kudos coming toward Cherokee because of their increased services to the region. The facilities got a face-lift and the employees go a boost in morale.

About ten months into the fiscal year the CFO started to notice that Cherokee was having cash flow problems. There was just barely enough money around to pay the employees. Payments to suppliers were being postponed. By the end of the fiscal year Cherokee was really strapped with creditors pounding on the door.

An end of the year analysis showed Cherokee had spent its $25M expense budget. Expenses were quite close to the plan. However, the revenue side was a disaster; Cherokee had taken in only $21M. The issue: $25M dollars had been spent – it couldn't be unspent. But now there was a $4M hole in Cherokee's finances.

The board, formerly a pass-through board, woke up and determined there was a significant problem. The board couldn't understand how things could get out of control. How did Cherokee spend more than its income? In a moment of anger, the board fired both the CFO and the CEO. The board's culture changed at that time to a more activist culture.

What happened next? The board chair went to a local patron and borrowed $4M in long-term debt. That got Cherokee through its immediate crisis. The board then hired a new CEO and CFO to take Cherokee into the future. One of the early activities of the new management team was to redo the budget into a more realistic budget, and to institute budget spending controls that tied spending to income. Cherokee still exists, is doing okay as a firm, and is gradually paying back the $4M it borrowed.

Discussion Questions

1. What system could Cherokee set up that would have tied expenditures to income?

2. Could Cherokee keep track of its income, expenses and budget on a monthly, weekly, or daily basis?

3. How should the board of a firm be involved in monitoring the budget?

4. How should the CEO be involved in monitoring the budget?

5. Should the board have fired the CEO and CFO? If so, why? If not, what alternative courses of action could the board have taken?

Analysis

What Cherokee did was not all that unusual. Revenue and expense budgets are developed, then enough revenues don't come in to support the expenditures. Various budget managers throughout the organization who don't have the big picture in mind go ahead and spend their expense allocation, leaving the entire firm high and dry when sufficient revenues fail to come in.

The Board of Directors, the CEO, and the CFO share responsibility for the significant bust of the budget. The Board of Directors through its finance committee should have been receiving and carefully reviewing monthly budget reports that give up-to-date information on revenues and expenses. The committee should have blown the whistle and required the firm to get its expenses in line with its revenues.

Similarly, the CEO should have regular reports of the finances. Like the Board of Directors, he should have called the shots to bring some sanity to the budget situation.

The CFO is the officer most directly responsible for budget health. The CFO should have developed policies that account for phasing of revenues and expenses and tied expenditures to revenues. The CFO should be reviewing the accounts at least weekly, and should have spotted the problem early in the fiscal year, early enough take some actions to correct the problems caused by the revenue shortfall.

The problem at Cherokee was so egregious, and the oversight that should have occurred so common-sense and relatively easy, that the Board needed to get a new CEO and CFO who would mind the store. In doing so, the Board needed to realize its own culpability in the budget mess.

Case 4.4 Counting the Cost Up Front

Weigs University (WU) of Texas was a private, not-for-profit university offering bachelor's, master's and doctoral degrees. Founded in 1897, the university in 2018 had 5400 degree-seeking students. WU had a good reputation in the area, was fully accredited, and had second-level accreditation in several professional disciplines. President of WU was Winston Murphy, who in 2018 had been president for eight years. In terms of annual finances, the school ran in the black, but its surpluses were largely non-existent, budgets were tight, and the university had only $500,000 in reserves.

WU's physical facilities were largely in good shape; there was little deferred maintenance on the campus. The 450-acre campus had considerable green space. There were excellent sports facilities for WU's basketball, football, baseball, soccer, swimming, and track and field programs.

One of WU's principal themes and values was Community. There were numerous academic and co-curricular activities that emphasized togetherness and strengthening of the community. Visitors to campus often commented on the family atmosphere on the campus.

President Murphy fully embraced the Community motif. There was one facility that WU did not have that Murphy thought would enhance the community aspects of life at WU, and that would be to have an auditorium big enough to hold all the members of the community for all-campus events.

After dreaming of such a facility for four years, Murphy went to the board and proposed a new auditorium facility. It would seat 6,000 people, would cost $30M, and would take 18 months to build once construction started. The board approved the project and gave Murphy the go-ahead to start fund-raising for the auditorium.

With the board's approval, Murphy and the university advancement staff started the silent phase of the campaign and raised $17M in the first 24 months. The campaign then went public and raised another $9M in the next 18 months. With $26M in hand or committed pledges, Murphy was anxious to get started with construction. With the board's approval the signal was given to move ahead. General and sub-contractors were signed up, ground-breaking took place after students arrived in the fall, and the building started up.

In August of the following year, about 12 months into the construction project, Murphy and WU's CFO realized that fund-raising had dried up and there was still a shortfall of $3M for the new building. Murphy was in a pickle, since there weren't funds available to complete the project. He was too far in to abandon the project, so he used some of the incoming fall tuition to pay for the remainder of the building. Unfortunately, that depleted a big chunk of the projected income for the year; the year closed with a $3M operating deficit.

The next year enrollment dropped by 200 students, with a consequent drop in revenues of a half-million dollars. That year the university closed its books with an operational debt of $1.4M. WU had to go to the bank and use short-term borrowing to meet payroll during the summer.

The following year enrollment dropped another 200 students, and the university incurred an operational debt of $1.1M. Reserves were depleted, and the university now had an accumulated operational debt of $5.5M.

Unfortunately for WU, the fourth year was the year WU had a scheduled visit from the regional accreditors. The accreditors took a look at the university's finances and put the university on probation because of its financial situation.

The board of directors looked for a scape-goat for the university's bad situation, and decided the scape-goat was Murphy. Murphy was asked to resign, he was paid $500,000 for the remaining two years on his contract, and a new president was brought in to try to bring the university back to financial health.

Discussion Questions

1. Should the board have approved moving ahead with the project when the funds were not completely available?

2. Why was Murphy so dead-set on moving ahead with the project before all the money had come in?

3. Did the accreditation organization make a good

decision when it put the university on probation?

4. Why did the board wait so long to take action against Murphy?

5. Should the board have bought out Murphy's contract, or should he have been fired for cause?

Analysis

This situation happens quite often in not-for-profit organizations. The CEO wants to build a new building, because that is one of the ways of gaining recognition by the stakeholders. He or she then plans the new facility, gets approval from the board to raise money for the project, and moves ahead. When there are funds for about four-fifths of the cost, the CEO gets antsy and wants to move ahead. The CEO assures the board that the funds will be coming in, either from additional gifts or new income that will be generated because of the new facility.

Before the project is finished the CEO realizes that the funds are not there to complete the facility, so the CEO dips into current funds for the completion money. That in turn reduces the operation funds and sets up a financial crisis for the institution. It may take several years for the university to dig itself out of the dungeon The CEO may or may not survive the debacle.

Case 4.5: Count the Change

HELP was a social service company based in Denver, Colorado. Its principal clients were the many homeless and indigent in the Denver area. HELP was a not-for-profit, 501(c)3 organization that had been in existence for 12 years. The director was Nelson Reed. HELP depended on support from donors to maintain its $4M annual budget.

Each Thursday night there was a HELP Booster meeting run by Reed. Typical attendance was 15-20 people. The meetings were similar in tone to the proverbial revival meeting. At each Booster meeting the attendants were given opportunity to donate to the cause. A typical financial take each week was about $750.

HELP's Treasurer was Jason Bisbee. Bisbee attended all the Booster meetings. Bisbee gathered the money each Thursday evening, then, since he was also the recording secretary, spent an hour or so each Friday morning recording the checks that came in from contributors, then deposited the receipts in the bank Friday afternoon.

One day Reed was in the bank talking to one of the tellers. The teller remarked that it was funny that HELP never had any currency in its weekly deposits. All that ever came in was checks. The teller remarked that every other business brought in both checks and currency.

The teller's comments made Reed curious about what was happening with the money that was coming in. Reed knew that there was currency coming in because he personally would contribute cash – typically a $10 or $20 bill. He had observed other donors putting in currency as well. Reed estimated the currency coming in each week to be in the $150-$200 range. So, what was happening to the currency?

After a few weeks Reed's curiosity got the best of him, so he told Bisbee what the teller had reported and asked Reed how that could be. Bisbee said the answer was simple. Each week Bisbee would count all the currency, then replace the currency with his personal check.

Over the next weeks Reed pondered Bisbee's story and wondered if Bisbee was taking some of the currency and not giving an equal amount in his personal replacement check.

As the calendar year was ending soon, Reed waited until the donors' contributions were tallied, then asked Bisbee for a list of the donors and their contribution amounts. Reed saw that Bisbee was recorded as having given $7250 for the year. Reed determined that if an average of $150 in currency was coming in each week from the Booster nights, then 50 weeks contributions would be $7,500. Reed concluded that Bisbee was not giving any of his own money to HELP; rather, he was replacing the cash with his personal checks and recording the amounts as his personal contribution.

Reed's trust in Bisbee was eroded. He called Bisbee in and asked Bisbee how much he had personally contributed to HELP the previous year. Bisbee said he had given $7250. Then Reed asked him about the currency that had come in; what happened to that money? By then Bisbee knew the jig was up, and he was caught in a lie. He said he didn't defraud HELP out of any of its money. What he was doing, he admitted, was claiming the $7250 on his tax return as a charitable contribution to HELP.

Reed did not fire Bisbee, nor did he report the problem to the IRS.

Discussion Questions

1. How should HELP have set up a system to count the incoming money?

2. What were the checks and balances to keep Bisbee honest?

3. Did HELP have any obligation to assure Bisbee was reporting his income accurately to the IRS?

4. What responsibility did Reed have in assuring all was good about handling and reporting the income?

5. How can small organizations like HELP ensure that proper internal controls with regard to handling currency and checks are implemented?

Analysis

Bisbee was not stealing from HELP, and HELP did not suffer any negative financial consequences due to Bisbee's actions. Bisbee was not ethical when he reported to the IRS, but HELP had no direct responsibility to the IRS.

Reed discovered that Bisbee had violated federal laws regarding reporting income to the IRS, but did not notify the IRS. Reed set himself up for charges from the IRS if Bisbee's actions were brought to light by the IRS.

There should always be at least two people involved in dealing with income to a firm. These two people are accountable to each other and each serves as a check on the other. Records should be made of each transaction and signed by both parties. Deposits to the bank and bank statements should be verified by both parties.

This system of dual handlers also protects the handlers. If someone accuses one of them for mishandling the funds, the other can serve as a witness that the funds were handled correctly.

Last, there should be an audit committee independent of the handlers who each year check on the system and assure that the policies and procedures are being carried out.

Case 4.6: End-Around Management

New to the position, the Executive Vice President at a small private university in the eastern region of the United States didn't understand why new issues kept coming up with the President. The EVP's portfolio of responsibilities was large and included academic affairs, student development, athletics, and enrollment, recruiting and marketing for both traditional students and adult students for a university of over 3,000 students. The EVP was considered second in command to the President and largely responsible for the operations of the university. He kept the President apprised of all projects and responsibilities during their regular monthly meetings and frequent drop-in meetings as needed. The EVP was an experienced manager having served at two other institutions previously for over twelve years in similar positions. The President came from another institution after a less than successful turnaround.

At first, the President and EVP seemed to be on the same page. The EVP felt like the outcomes of his decisions would be apparent as he implemented his ideas and directed his staff according to the goals for enrollment growth, academic excellence, and an excellent student experience he was tasked with achieving. The EVP was careful to understand the culture and move ahead with caution as needed. Soon it was apparent that the President must have alternative sources of information. Instead of expressing concerns and dealing directly with the EVP about the direction of various projects and responsibilities, the President had alternative perspectives and direct lobbying from those reporting to the EVP. In fact, the President met secretly with one of the EVP's direct reports for several months at a location off campus. In addition, several lower level staff members reporting to the EVP felt comfortable regularly going directly to the President when they didn't like the decisions or direction of the new EVP. Even though the EVP felt like he was transparent with the direction and reasons for his direction and decisions, the President never engaged in a conversation that indicated he preferred something different. When lower level staff expressed concerns, the President did not direct them back to the chain of command. At times, the EVP would receive questions or concerns from the President on various issues without benefit of the source or ability to follow up.

The EVP became aware of these end-arounds to the President when the President abruptly decided that one of the VP's would report directly to the President, effective immediately. There was no conversation ahead of time with the EVP letting him know of the structure change and the reasons behind the change. In fact, the EVP found out in a meeting where it was announced to the staff reporting to the EVP and VP. The new reporting relationship did not include sitting on the President's administrative team, further complicating the relationship between the EVP and VP.

Whenever any issue was questioned or clarity needed from the VP, email was the preferred method for communications; the VP would copy the president effectively ending any way forward for collaborative decision-making and alienating those trying to work together in solving problems and issues. The dysfunction of the reporting structure further divided the working relationships and provided the perfect environment for a lack of trust throughout the campus.

Discussion Questions

1. What could have the EVP done differently to work better with the President?

2. What could the President have done differently to work better with the EVP?

3. What should the President have done with people bypassing the reporting structure to speak directly to him?

4. What other strategies could have been used to build trust and improve decision-making?

5. Is it ever OK for employees or managers to break the established chain of command in an organization? If so, when?

Analysis

The CEO was seriously at wrong in this case. He did not use the firm's wiring diagram to his advantage.

He undercut his EVP by going around the EVP to the EVP's subordinates. He encouraged employees who reported to the EVP to jump over the EVP directly to him. The CEO even went so far as meeting secretly off campus with one of the EVP's direct reports.

The EVP seems to have kept in good practice with respect to the CEO by keeping the CEO informed about his work and thinking. The EVP should protest to the CEO about the communication and administrative structures and lack of trust in the organization.

At the end of the day, there has to be good communication between the management team of an organization. Communication channels should be wide open, and allow for upward, downward, and horizontal communication to flow freely. This is the best way to ensure there is trust among the management team.

Case 4.7: Count ALL of the Costs

Rogers University was a 4000-student, faith-based liberal arts college located in the suburbs of Montgomery, Alabama. The university was 135 years old, having been founded by northerners after the Civil War. It had a good reputation; its graduates did well in graduate schools around the country and in their various professions. As was typical of many private schools in the South, the university's budget was always on the edge. Some fiscal years ended with a few thousand dollars in surplus; in other years there was a small deficit. The president of the university was Ralph Kenton, a lawyer turned educator.

One loyal alumnus was Malcolm Sampson, a wealthy building contractor whose firm focused on large construction projects. Sampson got his start in business after earning a business degree at Rogers and having the support of two of his business professors.

Out of gratitude to Rogers and his education there, Sampson over a period of 15 years gave $90M to Rogers for construction of five large buildings on the campus. The buildings added to the attractiveness of the university, and helped the school maintain a steady enrollment while enrollments were dipping in other private schools in the region. Sampson passed away the year after the last large donation. It is noted that Sampson was a good friend of President Kenton.

Rogers used all $90M on the five construction projects. Over the years the university had been fortunate in not having to put much money into the buildings, so little maintenance funds were built into the budget. But now the buildings were old enough that more funds were required for maintenance and repairs. The oldest of the five buildings needed a new roof. In one building the central HVAC system failed. Now, all at once, the university faced a $5M immediate cost for repairs and maintenance on the new buildings. Further, a consultant suggested that the university should annually budget 4% of the costs of the buildings for regular upkeep and maintenance. Unfortunately, the university didn't have reserves for the immediate budget hit, nor plans for such a big permanent budget adjustment.

The university exercised its short-term borrowing privileges with a local bank and got enough funds for emergency repairs. However, the fiscal year ended with a $3.5M operational debt. The following year the university could still not balance its budget and ended with an accumulated operational debt of $8.5M.

Kenton had been president for 25 years during the period of Sampson's gifts. The University's Board of Trustees was a pass-through board that followed Kenton's lead on almost all matters. But after two years of increasing operational debt, the board woke up and decided that something needed to change. In particular, the Board determined that Kenton had misused the large gifts from Sampson and needed to go. Kenton was given a decent outgoing package, and was terminated.

Discussion Questions

1. How can an institution project ahead for facility maintenance and repairs?

2. Should the university have required a maintenance endowment for each building constructed, and included the amount of the endowment in the funds needs for the building?

3. Was Kenton wise in using all of Sampson's gifts for new buildings without building in funds for maintenance and repairs?

4. What was the responsibility of the architect to notify Rogers and Kenton about projected ongoing repairs and maintenance?

5. Did Kenton's personal friendship with Sampson color Kenton's decisions about the construction projects?

Analysis

Kenton made a common mistake when he built facilities – he didn't take into account the additional costs of maintaining, repairing, and updating the buildings over time. Many times, additional personnel will be required. Kenton added a significant fixed cost without providing an income stream to care for those costs.

Kenton could get by with that for a while, because the new building would probably not need significant repairs or maintenance for five or more years: no new roof, no new HVAC system, no new carpets, etc.

One university built a new campus with multiple

buildings. The big repairs did not occur for 20 years, then it was like the roof falling in. All at once there were massive costs to keep the buildings up and running.

Construction firms know about maintenance costs. There are standard figures available which can be used as projections on the costs of maintenance for years into the future. These projected costs should be used in deciding about whether and when to move ahead with a building project.

Case 4.8: Management by Hubris

Water parks are supposed to be a place for summer fun. They provide a great place for summer employment as well. When a water slide turns deadly…who is responsible? In the Kansas City area, a well-publicized case landed in court with owners, managers and employees being criminally charged with an unfortunate accident where a ten-year old child died on the Verrückt Water Slide in 2016. Although the criminal charges in this case will ultimately determine fault, are there some management failures that led to this tragic accident?

The hoopla for the new slide at the Schlitterbahn chain's water park opening located in Kansas City started during construction. The owners of the water park were part of a reality television show and were under pressure to have the slide ready for the show promoted as "the tallest and fastest water slide in the world." According to reports, the co-owner was asked by a team working on the Travel Channel's *Xtreme Waterparks* show to jointly work on the idea. The parties did not agree, and the co-owner along with a ride designer with the company decided to build the slide themselves. The owner really wanted the notoriety of the slide to help bring sales to the park.

According to CNN (Waterpark, 2018):

The water slide, named Verrückt which means "crazy or insane" in German, was designed for two to three riders to be strapped in a raft with a total weight between 400 and 500 pounds. The raft would then "slide down a jaw-

dropping 168-foot-7-inch structure, only to be blasted back up a second massive hill and then sent down yet another gut-wrenching 50-foot drop for the ultimate in water slide thrills," the park's website said. Riders on rafts reached speeds exceeding 70 mph.

With the urgency of the television show and the resulting publicity and after several postponements, the ride was officially opened on July 10, 2014 after being featured on the reality television show, *Xtreme Waterparks*. In addition, the ride was voted the "Best New Waterpark Ride" at the 2014 Golden Ticket Awards. For the first two years, the ride attracted such large crowds that riders were encouraged to make reservations.

Several injuries and problems were apparent from the early days of the ride; however, no corrective action was taken. Unfortunately, it took the death of a 10-year old child for the ride to be closed in 2016.

According to the indictment handed down in 2018, the owner and designer "lacked technical expertise to design a properly functioning water slide." They were also accused of not performing standard engineering procedures or tests on how the slide would perform. In their haste to launch the ride, they used "trial and error methods" to test the safety of the ride. Reports confirmed that the ride was poorly designed without any input from engineers or external government oversight (except for zoning issues) at the local or state levels. In fact, government officials were caught up in the publicity that the ride brought to the community.

Questions asked by the *Kansas City Star* newspaper in August 2016 included:

> *Was the design of the ride too aggressive? Did it bake in too many hard-to-control factors? Did late-stage changes pose added danger? Whose decision was it? Was Verrückt too much too fast?* (Design, 2016)

Discussion Questions

1. The owner was intimately involved with the design and promotion of the ride, but who is ultimately responsible for the decisions?

2. Did the hubris of the television reality show allow for poor decision-making or the time needed for a comprehensive safety analysis?

3. What is the role of government oversight in this case?

4. What management decisions could have prevented this tragic death?

5. What are some strategies to help managers maintain good risk management practices while still taking risks that may result in business growth?

Analysis

When customer safety is involved, do not be in a hurry to move a project ahead. Take time to carefully consider all factors that might provoke an injury to a customer, and mitigate the problems that are revealed.

The leaders of an organization should realize from the beginning that they don't have all the answers to the organization's challenges. There will be individuals in the organization who have expertise in various matters and those persons should be consulted.

If there are technical matters that need to be resolved, then calling in outside experts is in order. The recommendations of these outside experts should be seriously considered and implemented where possible.

Leaders should be especially concerned when customer safety is being considered. Here it is always good to have an outside group assure the organization that everything is in order to protect customer safety. By following the recommendations of the outside firm, the organization may head off lawsuits if there is an injury to a customer.

Case 4.9: Micro-Managing for Failure

A faith-based university located in the southwest found itself with its twelfth straight year of operational losses. An experienced CEO came out of retirement and was put in place seven years prior with a stated plan to turn the university around in five years. Everyone expected that the CEO would be directive given the gravity of the situation, and the campus warmly welcomed him and his ideas. However, after six more years of operational losses with little visible improvement by the majority of the campus, the campus wanted answers. Each year, the CEO had an explanation for the surprises that kept the university from making a profit. The explanations were wearing thin with the campus; however, the board seemed to accept the rationale with little questioning. After the sixth year of operational losses, the board extended a new five-year contract to the CEO, much to the surprise of the campus.

Justification from the CEO each year would include any number of explanations: an unexpected increase in the amount of scholarships, an unexpected decrease in enrollment, a major investment in online and non-traditional programs that did not yield increased enrollment, a string of consultants that yielded no major increases in revenue while adding significant expenses, among others.

The CEO's management team did not operate as a functional team. The CEO was the gatekeeper for all agenda items and was the sole approval for any major initiatives on campus. While the administrative team "voted," no hard questions were discussed extensively if there was perceived defensiveness by the CEO. If the CEO approved of the initiative, it would pass and if he did not, it would either not come up for a vote or the CEO would lead the discussion accordingly.

The CEO was also defensive about the non-traditional enrollment area and scholarship increases for student athletes. To add to the dysfunction, the CEO typically managed decisions 2-3 levels below the vice presidents put in place to provide leadership. If decisions by a vice president did not align with the CEO's preferences, there was no discussion to try and come to a mutual agreeable solution. Instead, the CEO would order his changes at multiple levels. This was evident across campus and a cause for concern, particularly when curriculum decisions were on the line.

At the latest board meeting, the CEO tried to manage the narrative and tried to keep the negative comments or questions from reaching the board. Vice presidents typically invited to the executive committee of the board were also excluded. The negativity was managed once again, and the board meeting ended uneventfully. Although an improvement, the projected operational loss of over one million dollars ($30 million total budget) is expected which brings to eight years of losses during the CEO's tenure.

Discussion Questions

1. During a turnaround situation, what are the measures a board should use for success of a CEO?

2. Did the Board exercise its due diligence in following up on the continued operational losses?

3. What is the CEO's purview in a turnaround situation? What is the role of the vice presidents?

4. Would the campus have a different reaction to the CEO's leadership style if they provided an operational surplus?

5. What are some of the consequences of a manager that does not follow the established chain of command?

Analysis

The CEO was at major fault in this university. He was a micro-manager who did not trust the work of his direct reports. If he did not like their work, he should have replaced them with people he could trust.

It was a poor use of the CEO's time to micro-manage his direct reports. He should have been working on strategic issues rather than getting so involved in the day-to-day running of the operation.

The CEO's team did not operate as a team. Rather than discuss matters in depth and then making a group decision, they kowtowed to the ideas of the CEO.

The Board of Trustees was at fault by not requiring the CEO's direct reports to talk directly to the Board. The Board was also at fault by keeping the CEO in position many years after it was clear the budget was not doing well. The Board acted more as a pass-through board than an active board.

Case 4.10: The Future Comes Quickly

Jeffrey Ellington was the President and CEO of a large national non-profit corporation, HelpUp Associates. HelpUp provided an array of services to persons below or at the poverty line; the various services were designed to assist with all aspects of day-to-day living, allow personal advancement, and move recipients toward self-sufficiency. HelpUp had a very large staff, with hundreds of employees around the country, tens of thousands of patrons, donors and other stakeholders, and a budget in the high-tens of millions of dollars. HelpUp received no governmental support, and relied on donations, both corporate and individual. The reputation of the non-profit was excellent, and that reputation resulted in significant donations that allowed the firm to operate at a high level.

Ellington was an experienced businessman who had moved into the non-profit arena after an early retirement from the corporate world. He had been with HelpUp for many years. His business skills were superb, but he was somewhat old-fashioned when it came to technology. Ellington still used dictation and a secretary to create documents. When he heard the word "Instagram" he thought it was something from Western Union.

One HelpUp employee was a thirty-something, mid-level management team member in the Communications Department, Thomas Pell. Pell had nominal responsibility for online communication, including blogs and social media. Pell was extremely personable and quite witty. He was articulate, outgoing, well-liked among many donors and stakeholders, and he had many friends in the HelpUp community.

Ellington was aware of Pell's role, but was content to leave that area of responsibility to Pell. In fact, Ellington had only a very superficial knowledge of the arena of blogs and social media. At an intellectual level he somehow knew that such communication channels were important, but in reality, he had no real idea as to how they helped the organization.

After some time, Ellington started to hear certain rumors about Pell. The rumors came slowly at first but then accelerated; they came from all directions: staff, donors, patrons, and perhaps most importantly, members of the HelpUp Board of Directors. The rumors indicated that Pell was bad-mouthing the organization, bad-mouthing its mission, bad-mouthing its philosophy, and bad-mouthing its leadership. Rumors persisted and grew. Ellington began to accumulate stories of donors who declined to give support to HelpUp because of Pell's activity. He came to realize that HelpUp was losing staff members because of what Pell was doing. He soon concluded that Pell was a serious problem for the company, a problem that was rapidly growing.

Ellington inquired at the HelpUp human resources department and learned that a prior CEO had given Pell a five-year rolling contract that provided that at any point in time Pell could be terminated only "for cause" or with five-years notice.

A short time later, Ellington concluded that the damage being done by Pell was too great. His first response was to talk to Pell and offer him a settlement to leave. Pell's demands in response were outrageous and Pell refused to negotiate at a reasonable level.

Ellington then terminated Pell, and cited Pell's activity as "cause" for the termination. It was unclear that the things being done by Pell constituted actual contractual "cause," but Ellington determined that the worst that could happen would be that a court would find that he breached the contract. He was convinced that the actual damages that Pell could prove in court were far less than the amount of his settlement demands. Ellington prepared for litigation.

Pell did indeed hire an attorney, but his response was not a lawsuit. As Ellington waited for the litigation that was never to come, he started getting feedback from the same folks who had warned him about Pell's misconduct: staff, donors, patron, and members of his Board of Directors.

And this is what Ellington learned as he followed up on the information he was receiving from others: Pell had unleashed a deluge of harmful material on the internet. Pell was flooding blogs, emails, tweets, texts, and articles and discussions on a number of popular social media sources. The campaign was all directed squarely at Ellington. The various sources discussed what a wonderful employee Pell had been in speaking truth about the shortcomings of the organization, how unfairly he had been treated, how prejudiced Ellington was against him, and it then repeated all of the criticisms that had started the feud between Pell and Ellington in the first place.

At first, Ellington did not understand what was happening or how potent the campaign might become. Then he started to get phone calls and emails, texts and Facebook messages. All were directed against him. And they came on like a firestorm. His family members started to be aware of what was happening. Facebook pages were created just to oppose his leadership at HelpUp and they contained message after message of scathing attack. Ellington's wife and children were extremely upset.

Ellington's first strategy was an attempt to reply to and refute the content of the various messages, but he soon found that responding only garnered more and more heated responses. The discussion boards turned out not to be places for reasoned discourse or debate. The constant attack distracted him and caused his performance as the non-profit's leader to suffer. He then tried to ignore the attacks, but the impact on Ellington and on his family was undeniable. This continued for months as the online attacks on Twitter, Facebook Instagram, and other outlets did not let up.

Eventually, the Chairman of the Board of HelpUp stepped in and negotiated a settlement with Pell. And eventually, the firestorm died down. Ellington's tenure as President and CEO did not last long after this incident.

Discussion Questions

1. How does a senior executive understand or address the issue of generational differences in responses to adversity?

2. What are some of the ways that "public outcry" such as in this case can damage an organization or a leader?

3. What steps might Ellington have taken besides terminating Pell?

4. How can someone such as Ellington avoid being surprised by emerging technologies and the manners in which they are used?

5. What steps should any company take when there is an online and social media attack against the company or its leadership?

6. If you were in Ellington's place when the online attack commenced, what would you have done differently?

Analysis

There is an old saying that "if it ain't broke, don't fix it." Many managers have come over the many years of a long career to understand and use certain business tools. If those tools are working for the manager, there may be a tendency to continue to use those tools without real regard for what new tools are developing that might be better or different. This can lead to a certain blindness to the possible impact of new technology.

This is very much true in the arena of business

communication. For those who entered business before the end of the last (twentieth) century, there were a relatively limited array of business communication channels: letters, phones, telegraph, fax.

Then the internet evolved and electronic communication channels blossomed: text, email, LinkedIn, Facebook, Twitter, YouTube, Instagram, intranets, cell, mobile and smart phones, Skype, Adobe Connect, web sites, chat rooms, discussion boards, and many others. To some degree there is still layering of understanding, and use of these channels varies according to various demographics (age, education, experience, geographic).

In this case, Ellington perceived an HR problem that was adversely impacting the non-profit for which he was responsible. He was saddled with a restrictive contract that limited his options. He charted a course to solve the problem that was consistent with his experience and knowledge. It involved risk of litigation, but Ellington presumed that he understood and could manage that particular risk. In a very real sense, everything he did was reasoned and reasonable.

Ellington had a blind spot. Unfortunately, he did not understand the weaponization of certain communication channels. The channels are newer and are more in the realm of Pell, who did understand. Pell had no need for litigation: he had a different strategy.

It can be difficult to see the future coming at you. Arguably, Ellington did nothing wrong given his perception and his perspective. He was simply blind to a strategy that was not within his sphere of vision.

Companies and leaders today need to understand that

with every change in technology, communication risks and strategies need to evolve. A company needs to be ready with a plan before an internet onslaught occurs. The science of crisis communication must evolve with the technology, and sometimes the technological changes can sneak up on an executive.

Pell was able to inflict pain on Ellington because Ellington did not see it coming. Every executive suite needs access to reliable expertise and information about new technologies (on a day-to-day basis), the uses of the technologies (good and bad) and effective responses. This may include the cost a specific senior employee expert on staff. Alternatively, it may require a retainer contract with an outside group specializing in such matters.

And it is equally important to understand that attacks such as in this case can last a very long time. In that sense, it will often require patience and resolution to outlast the attacks.

Case 4.11: Three Pass-Through Boards

In the past seven years one of the authors audited the work of three not-for-profit organizations that got into financial trouble. It is good to report that two of the three have turned around and are doing well; the third did not make it.

The three organizations were similar in several ways. They were relatively small, with annual revenues of less than $50M. Each had been in existence for over 50 years; one for more than one hundred years. They had good reputations and were doing good work. The employees were committed to their respective missions. They had decent physical facilities.

Another big similarity was the board structure. In each case there was a pass-through board consisting of friendly individuals who saw themselves as sometime-consultants to the CEO. Each board had a small executive committee. The boards came into town occasionally and conducted the legally required business following an agenda developed largely by the CEO and approved by the board chair. The board was dependent on the organizations' officers for reports and interpretations of reports.

The CEOs were also similar. In each case the CEO had risen through the mission ranks and was not trained in business management. The CEO depended on the CFO for insight into the business and financial operations of the organization. The organizations did not pay outstanding salaries, so depended on people of good will and mission commitment to fill the employee ranks.

Each successive CEO was impressed by the employees and empowered those employees who also shared a deep drive for mission fulfillment. Further, in each case the CEO did not like to make hard decisions about people and product.

So over time the finances got rough. Income was lower than expenses. The organizations' savings accounts were gradually depleted and the organizations started to run in the red. Eventually things ran off the rails and the CFO and CEO had to take decisive action. The CEOs reported to the board how bad a shape their organizations were in. In all three cases it was a surprise to the board chairs and to board members.

Emergency meetings of the boards were called, and in all three cases, the CEOs and CFOs were let go with decent exit packages. The board chairs effectively became the CEOs of their respective organizations.

Searches were started and new CEOs and CFOs employed. This time the searches focused on getting people in place who had business knowledge and experience, and personalities who could make tough decisions, as well as having commitment to the organizational mission. The new leaders were able to come in to make several significant decisions concerning personnel and product, and begin to make a turn-around in finances. Two of the three did solve their problems; one failed and closed.

The biggest change in the two remaining companies was the work of the boards of directors. No longer are the boards pass-through boards. The boards have taken charge of their respective organizations. In each case the boards have picked several new members who have business and legal experience. The boards now meet bi-monthly in extended meetings, have undergone several board training workshops, and are now collecting their own data and information independent of the CEOs and CFOs. The trauma was deep, but at least two of these fine institutions were salvaged.

Discussion Questions

1. Could the boards have organized themselves in such a way that the bad shape of the finances would not have caught them by surprise?

2. How does a mission-driven organization protect itself from being exclusive and closed off to new ideas and influence?

3. How long should a board let the organization run in the red before taking decisive action?

4. Should the board have a finance committee to provide oversight to the work of the CEO and the CFO?

5. How can boards ensure that board members understand their roles and responsibilities prior to committing to serve?

Analysis

Management failure can be attributed to the boards of the three organizations. The culture of the boards was pass-through. Board members did not see themselves as caretakers of the organization and just let matters flow without exercising due diligence.

There should have been a finance committee that provided oversight about the finances. This committee should demand regular reports from the CFO concerning the state of the finances, together with projections of future income and expenses, and with recommendations how to correct any inadequacies in funding.

The work of the board of trustees is critical to the success of any organization. Gone are the days where boards can be passive – pass-through boards. Boards must actively engage in the business of the organization, and take their governance and stewardship roles seriously.

This page intentionally left blank

CHAPTER FIVE

MANAGEMENT FAILURE REPRIEVE

This page intentionally left blank

17 Reasons Why Businesses Fail (Norris Limbani)

1. Poor Management
2. Starting A Business for The Wrong Reason
3. Lack of Planning
4. Insufficient Capital
5. Overexpansion
6. Obsession with Cutting Costs
7. Inventory Mismanagement
8. Cash Flow Problems
9. Lack of Records or Data
10. Mishandling of A Delinquent Bank Debt Situation
11. Customer Concentration
12. Supplier Concentration
13. Maintaining Out-Dated Processes and Activities
14. Wrong Location
15. Lack of Employee Management and Engagement
16. Choosing the Wrong Partner
17. Lack of a Resilient Attitude

In addition to the reasons Limbani gave, there are several other reasons why management fails. These include:

18. Personal Moral Lapse

19. Board Fails to Investigate

20. CEO Fails to Investigate

21. Violation of Company Policy

22. Failure to Act in Timely Way

23. Failure to Take Short-Term Risk

24. Failure to Take Long-Term Risk

25. Keeping Mediocre Employees in Place

26. Company Policy Hinders Good Decisions

27. Company Culture Hinders Good Decisions

28. Sexual Harassment or Hostile Work Environment

29. Failure to Determine Market

RESOURCES

The sources listed here were either referenced in this book or are recommended to the reader for further study on business and management.

Brandon, J. (2017, June 17.). Myers-Briggs just discovered there is a personality type for entrepreneurs. Retrieved December, 2020 from https://www.inc.com/john-brandon/myers-briggs-just-discovered-there-is-a-personality-type-for-entrepreneurs.html

Bringing job seekers and recruiters together (n.d.). *The Recruiter Network*. Retrieved May 27, 2021 from https://www.therecruiternetwork.com/recruiter/index.php?source=gs-er-o3er-atwwop&gclid=EAIaIQobChMIzKDHmc6b7wIVeyGtBh0qTw4BEAAYAiAAEgJ6a_D_BwE

Builders with risk talent: Eagerly embracing challenges. (2017, April 25). *Gallup*. Retrieved from https://www.gallup.com/cliftonstrengths/en/250274/builders-risk-talent-eagerly-embracing-challenges.aspx

Caddell, J. (n.d.). Why the divorce rate is higher among entrepreneurs. Retrieved May 27, 2021 from https://mybestrelationship.com/divorce-rates-higher-among-entrepreneurs/

Cahn, N. (2017, October 16). A closer look at the jobs with the highest and lowest divorce rates. *Institute for Family Studies*. Retrieved from https://ifstudies.org/blog/a-closer-look-at-the-jobs-with-the-highest-and-lowest-divorce-rates

Cautious vs. risk-taker: Personality traits at work. (n.d.). *Hire Success*. Retrieved May 27, 2021 from https://www.hiresuccess.com/help/cautious-vs-risk-taker-personality-types-at-work

Cohen, W.A. (2013). *Drucker on marketing*. New York: McGraw-Hill.

Crewson, P.E. (1997, October). Public-service motivation: Building empirical evidence of incidence and effect. *Journal of Public Administration Research and Theory*, *7*(4), 499-518. https://doi.org/10.1093/oxfordjournals.jpart.a024363

Denning, S. (2018). *The age of agile*. New York: Amarylis Business.

Doz, Y., Santos, J., & Williamson, P. (2001). *From global to metanational*. Boston: Harvard.

Drucker, P. (1954). *The practice of management*. New York: Harper Collins.

Entrepreneur personality. (n.d.). *16Personalities*. Retrieved May 27, 2021 from https://www.16personalities.com/estp-personality

Freiberg, K. & Freiberg, J. (1996). *NUTS: Southwest Airlines' crazy recipe for business and personal success.* Portland, OR: Bard Press.

Frey, R., Richter, D., Schupp, J., Hertwig, R., & Mata, R. (2021). Identifying robust correlates of risk preference: A systematic approach using specification curve analysis. *Journal of Personality and Social Psychology, 120*(2), 538-557.

Gardner, M., & Steinberg, L. (2005). Peer influence on risk taking, risk preference, and risky decision making in adolescence and adulthood: An Experimental Study. *Developmental Psychology 41*(4), 625-635.

Ghosh, P. (2021, March 1). Top 10 applicant tracking systems (ATS) software for 2021. Retrieved from https://www.toolbox.com/hr/recruitment-onboarding/articles/top-applicant-tracking-systems/

Goldratt, E. (1999). *Theory of constraints.* Great Barrington, MA: North River Press.

Goran, J., LaBerge, L., & Srinivasan, R. (2017, July). Culture for a digital age. *McKinsey Quarterly.* Retrieved from https://lediag.net/wp-content/uploads/2018/05/0-Culture-for-a-digital-age.pdf

Harter, J. & Askins, A. (2015, April). What great managers do to engage employees. *Harvard Business Review.* Retrieved from https://hbr.org/2015/04/what-great-managers-do-to-engage-employees

Hedges, K. (2013). The secret to effective one-on-one meetings with direct reports. *Forbes,* November 11. Retrieved from https://www.forbes.com/sites/work-in-progress/2013/11/11/the-secret-to-effective-one-on-one-meetings-with-direct-reports/#22a8829b4687

Hofstede, G., Hofstede, G.J., & Minkov, M. (2010). *Cultures and organizations: Software of the mind.* New York: McGraw-Hill.

Hsee, C.K., & Weber, E.U. (1997). A fundamental prediction error: Self-others discrepancies in risk preference. *Journal of Experimental Psychology: General 126*(1), 45-53. Retrieved from https://www.apa.org/pubs/journals/xge/

Kaplan, R.S. & Mikes, A. (2012). Managing risks: A new framework. *Harvard Business Review, 90*(6), 48-60. Retrieved from https://hbr.org/2012/06/managing-risks-a-new-framework

Keinan, R. & Bereby-Meyer, Y. (2017). Perceptions of active versus passive risks, and the effect of personal responsibility. *Personality and Social Psychology Bulletin, 43*(7), pp. 999-1007.

Knight, R. (2016, August 8). How to make your one-on-ones with employees more productive. *Harvard Business Review.* Retrieved from https://hbr.org/2016/08/how-to-make-your-one-on-ones-with-employees-more-productive

Lawler III, E.E., & Worley C.G. (2006). *Built to change.* San Francisco: Jossey-Bass.

McGregor, L., & Doshi, N. (2015, November 25). How company culture shapes employee motivation. *Harvard Business Review.* Retrieved from https://hbr.org/2015/11/how-company-culture-shapes-employee-motivation

Mintzberg, H., Ahlstand, B., & Lampel, J. (2005). *Strategy safari.* New York: Free Press.

Newstrom, J., & Davis, K. (2002). *Organizational behavior: Human behavior at work.* New York: McGraw Hill.

Risk analysis and risk management: Assessing and managing risk. (n.d.). *MindTools.* Retrieved May 27, 2021 from https://www.mindtools.com/pages/article/newTMC_07.htm

Robbins, S.P., & DeCenzo, D.A. (2007). *Supervision Today!* Upper Saddle River, NJ: Pearson/Prentice Hall.

Storm, S. (2018, October 13). Here's how much of a risk-taker you are, based on your personality type. *Psychology Junkie.* Retrieved from https://www.psychologyjunkie.com/2018/10/13/heres-how-much-of-a-risk-taker-you-are-based-on-your-personality-type/

Toffler, A. (1970). *Future shock.* New York: Bantam.

Tracy, B. (2017). Learning leadership: Eight key skills that make an effective manager. *Forbes,* March 13. Retrieved from https://www.forbes.com/sites/forbescoachescouncil/2017/03/13/learning-leadership-eight-key-skills-that-make-an-effective-manager/#2e22bf621354

Vlaev, I., Wright, N., Dolan, P., Wallace, B., Nicolle, A., & Dolan, R. (2017). Other people's money: The role of reciprocity and social uncertainty in decisions for others. *Journal of Neuroscience, Psychology, and Economics 10*(2/3), 59-80. Retrieved from https://www.apa.org/pubs/journals/npe

Whalen, E.L. (1991). *Responsibility center budgeting.* Bloomington, IN: Indiana University.

Winseman, A.L., Clifton, D.O., & Liesveld, C. (2004). *Living your strengths* (2nd ed.). New York: Gallup.

Womack, J.P. & Jones, D.T. (2003). *Lean thinking* (2nd ed.). New York: Free Press.

THE AUTHORS

Joshua Jensen, Associate Professor of Leadership, was named Dean of the College of Business at Northwest Nazarene University in Nampa, Idaho, United States in 2022. Jensen is a seasoned business leader and leadership consultant with a longstanding career that spans many industries including higher education, K-12 education, non-profit healthcare, local government, and the private sector. He holds an EdD degree in organizational leadership as well as MBA and MPA degrees. He also holds certification through the Society for Human Resource Management as a Senior Certified Professional (SHRM-SCP). Jensen is active in business research with several publications in business and management journals as well as several books related to management and leadership.

For fun Jensen likes to spend time with his family and serve in various capacities at his church. He has been married to Amelia for 28 years and they have four grown children and three grandchildren.

Samuel Dunn is Professor of Business and Senior Fellow at Northwest Nazarene University in Nampa, Idaho, United States. Dunn holds a PhD degree in mathematics and a DBA degree in international business. Dunn served as Professor of Mathematics and Business, Dean, and Vice President for Academic Affairs at Seattle Pacific University, then Professor of Business and Mathematics and Vice President for Academic Affairs at Northwest Nazarene University. He is a long-time futurist with several publications in futurist journals. Dunn views himself as a businessperson working in the second largest civilian industry in the United States: education.

For fun Dunn likes to travel, read, and take Saturday trips with his wife, Lois. At the time of this writing he has been in 54 countries. The Dunns have two grown children; one is a forensic scientist and the other is a medical doctor, both living in the United States.

William (Bill) Russell retired in 2022 as the Dean of the College of Business at Northwest Nazarene University in Nampa, Idaho, United States. Russell is an attorney (civil trial attorney), a professor (business law and business ethics), a businessman and an ordained pastor. He earned a JD from the University of Denver (1975), an MBA from Regis University (2005), a Graduate Certificate in Christian Theology from Asbury Theological Seminary (2006), and he is ordained in the Church of the Nazarene (2014). He has created, operated and sold three companies. He has consulted for over 95 global and entrepreneurial businesses and organizations. He consults, writes and speaks on issues of Business Law, Business Ethics, Leadership, Advanced Negotiation, Business Education, and his favorite topic: Thinking like Warren Buffett. In 2010, Russell was awarded the International Business Teaching award (bestowed on one professor annually) by the Accreditation Council of Business Schools and Programs.

Russell has visited 51 countries globally and 49 states (North Dakota still awaits!). He and his wife, Nancy, have been married for 41 years and have two grown daughters and four grandchildren.

This page intentionally left blank

www.ingramcontent.com/pod-product-compliance
Lightning Source LLC
Chambersburg PA
CBHW072017060426
42446CB00044B/2758

* 9 7 8 1 7 3 6 6 3 1 8 5 0 *